Try some of these wonderful ideas from the Sidetracked Sisters!

• Attach a scratch pad and pen to yourself as you start reorganizing your kitchen. Then you'll know where everything goes and everything went.

• Hang your produce in plastic bags in the refrigerator. The vegetables and fruits will stay crisp, in view, and easy to get at—not crumpled and forgotten at the back of the crisper drawer.

• Tape a table-of-contents card to the inside of each kitchen drawer to help keep things in their new places—and to keep the drawers from getting scrambled by frantic utensil-seekers.

• Organize your leftovers. Double-wrap them immediately for the freezer, label them, and file the information under "Crisis" in your card file. Thaw them when an emergency arises.

• Use the kids as coupon cutters. Have them gather the products from supermarket shelves while you shop, and pay them for their efforts from the "cents off."

With lots more hints like these—plus the fun of the Sidetracked Glossary, the family photo album, and episodes from their daily life—Pam and Peggy will keep you laughing as you learn how to *Catch-Up on the Kitchen* yourself.

D0188007

Also by

PAM YOUNG & PEGGY JONES

Sidetracked Home Executives

Published by
WARNER BOOKS

The Sidetracked Sisters
Catch-Up on the Kitchen

PAM YOUNG & PEGGY JONES

WARNER BOOKS

A Warner Communications Company

Warner Books Edition

Copyright © 1983 by Pam Young and Peggy Jones

All rights reserved.

Warner Books, Inc.
666 Fifth Avenue
New York, N.Y. 10103

 A Warner Communications Company

Printed in the United States of America
First printing: April 1983

10 9 8 7 6 5 4 3

Book design by Richard Oriolo

Library of Congress Cataloging in Publication Data

Young, Pam.
    The sidetracked sisters catch-up on the kitchen.

    1. Home economics. 2. Kitchens. 3. Cookery. 4. Housewives—Time
management. I. Jones, Peggy. II. Rosen, Sydney Craft. III. Title.
TX158.Y63 1983   641.3   82-21846
ISBN 0-446-37526-8 (USA)
ISBN 0-446-37549-7 (Canada)

Dedicated with more love to Fred

SPECIAL THANKS

Special thanks to DANNY, MOM and DAD, MIKE, PEGGY, CHRIS, JOANNA, JEFF, and ALLYSON. Without their love and support, this book would not have been possible.

CONTENTS

Introduction 1

1. From Pigpen to Paradise 3
2. Confessions from Paradise 15
3. Neat v. Eat...24
4. Sidetrackers Beware 31
5. The Best Laid Plans Are for the Birds 36
6. Plan Your Work and Eat Your Plan................43
7. Starting Over...56
8. Maintenance 79
9. This Little Piggy Went to Market 93
10. Guess Who's Coming to Dinner—
    Old Mr. Leftover 104
11. Pigging Out..109
12. The Harvest Martyr...117
13. Sidetracked and Single 126
14. Trouble at the Trough 135
15. The Heart of the Home 145

Appendix...155
Recipes...176

The Sidetracked Sisters
Catch-Up on the Kitchen

INTRODUCTION

We've been very happy about and grateful for the response to our first best-selling book, *Sidetracked Home Executives.*™ The number of copies sold has been impressive, however, we know the truth. Four out of five people who purchased the book had to purchase it again because they either: (1) lost it; (2) lent it to someone, and they forgot whom; or (3) wrecked it by leaving it on the kitchen counter when a chicken was thawing.

We've wondered if maybe this second book about the kitchen should have been included as Part II of our first book. Then we'd have had one of those thick volumes that your toddler sits on when he's outgrown the high chair and is still too short to sit at the table. Unfortunately, we hadn't figured out what to do with our kitchens when we wrote the first book about home organization. The kitchen is an advanced concept, and we weren't ready to talk about it until just recently.

After two years of concentration on food, we have unlocked the secret of efficiency in the kitchen. What we learned we have presented here from a reformed slob's point of view.

We have devised a menu-planning and kitchen maintenance system that will work for you whether you're a single parent, a senior citizen, a trapeze artist, or a flight attendant. The system will work for the wife or husband of a farmer, a minister, or a charter fisherman. It will even work for you if you are married to an orthodontist, have three kids, one dog, two cats, and a condo on the coast. The bottom line is ... if you eat at home, you need this book.

We recommend that you read *The Sidetracked Sisters Catch-Up on the Kitchen* all the way through before you set up the system. Once you have the feeling that the kitchen is the heart of the home, you'll be ready to go back to chapters seven and eight and get organized.

If you laughed with us in our first book, you'll like *The Sidetracked Sisters Catch-Up on the Kitchen,* too. You will see yourself in our experiences, and you'll be as excited as we were to gain control of your kitchen.

God bless your home and your family ... and God bless your kitchen, too.

1

FROM PIGPEN TO PARADISE

We have wonderful memories of starting the day when we were children. A crisp, chilly morning, the hint of smoke from a wood fire, the unmistakable scent of pancakes and hot maple syrup, can send us straight back in memory to the old family farmhouse.

The house was built in the 1800s. In winter it was heated with a fireplace in the living room. A previous owner, unable to stand the cold, had installed electric wall heaters in the bathroom and kitchen. The rest of the house, including our upstairs bedroom, was freezing.

We shared a double bed. With the first frost Mom would replace the sheets with flannel sheet-blankets, eliminating the icy shock of ironed percale. We slept on a mattress covered with a feather tick. Snug under several wool blankets and a down comforter, we would sink into a cozy warmth and fall asleep.

In the morning the irresistible aroma of bacon or sausage and sweet rolls would pull us gently from our covers into the harsh reality of a winter morning. We'd race across the freezing floor in our bare feet and dash down the wooden

stairs to the kitchen. Once through the sliding door between the hall and the kitchen, we knew how Sergeant Preston must have felt as he and Yukon King quickly entered their cabin, leaving the blinding blizzard outside. If Mrs. Preston—his mother—was anything like our mom, she'd have been waiting at the door with a couple of short stacks and a rasher of Canadian bacon.

Our mom was always there. She always had the table set before we came downstairs, and we never missed a day without orange juice. Our mom even looks like Anita Bryant. The kitchen was our family gathering place, where we lingered after meals, enjoying the companionship. It was our favorite room because it represented love, friendship, good food, and warmth. Even now, when we both have homes with central heating, we are drawn instinctively into our kitchens early in the morning in search of that warmth. The kitchen means far more to us than just a room with food.

Our childhood home was filled with love. As sisters growing up together, we found life to be one great adventure. There was only one slug in our path: We were messes. Our bedroom was a disgrace. We undressed and left weeks of clothing on beds, on chairs, and scattered across the floor.

We were thankful that we both could function in chaos and that we were equally chaotic. We've heard of sisters who have drawn Mason-Dixon-type lines when forced to be roommates, but sharing a room was a joy for us.

Neither of us was offended, visually or functionally, by the other's mess. Within the clutter there was respect, because we knew we both cared about our stuff; we just didn't hang it up. The Mason-Dixon liners have a real challenge. They have to deal with the obvious contrast, which in turn creates conflict.

Fights start when opposites live together and try to change each other. When one roommate is organized and the other is sidetracked, there are accusations and apologetic excuses, questions and explanations, demands and promises, expectations and disappointments. If both sides are willing to compromise, each recognizing the other's good, they can take advantage of their differences and grow.

Since we didn't have any differences to put aside, we lived in chaotic bliss. We had places to go, people to see, and so much in common. The mess was something we left Mom to worry about. And worry she did. She read every book on how to handle the messy child, and she wondered where she'd gone wrong with us. We think she considered our room the challenge of her life.

On a one-to-ten scale of order, we were a minus two. Our poor mom. She was at least a nine. She had no one to turn to for answers. She resorted to throwing once-a-week fits that prodded us into straightening up our pigpen. But the next day we'd fall back into our old ways. It wasn't until later, after marriage and six kids—three each—that we hit bottom. By then we had to get organized or disappear under mounds of soiled laundry, stacks of dirty dishes, and piles of unanswered mail.

Since we came from an unusually happy home, it probably was no surprise to anyone that we wanted to be homemakers. We wanted to recreate for our own families the same joy we had grown up with. In the beginning we struggled to follow the path carved out for us in high school home economics. But Miss Cratsberry never mentioned how to handle pails of dirty diapers, or to remove quickly the cat hairs that cover the police uniform of a late-to-work husband, or to arrange a bouquet of dandelions with quarter-inch stems, or to stay up all night with a sick child and still be flirtatious and attractive in the morning. There was a lot Miss Cratsberry didn't tell us—probably because Miss Cratsberry wasn't Mrs. Cratsberry.

We wished we had learned how to do income tax; instead she taught us how to make tailor tacks. She showed us how to baste an entire dress, instead of how to dress and baste an entire turkey. We practiced to perfection the art of entering and exiting an automobile with grace and ease. What she neglected to cover was how to sit stylishly on a three-hour, nonstop car trip to one's in-laws, with a wet baby on one's lap and two crazy toddlers strapped in the backseat, while engaging in clever conversation with a husband who was on automatic pilot.

With Miss Cratsberry as our home ec teacher, and our mom as our model of the perfect homemaker, we weren't prepared for the struggle of managing our own households. Reared in an immaculate home, where our mom organized and managed everything so perfectly, we assumed it had all been effortless. In our naiveté we'd wondered what Mom did all day while we were in school. Needless to say, we were shocked to discover the overwhelming responsibilities we had undertaken when we married. When you say "till death us do part," you don't realize how close that comes sometimes.

Our careers as homemakers went from shock to struggle. With the birth of each child, we fell deeper and deeper into the sea of clutter and chaos. Through those years, in an attempt to bail out of our mess, we read every book on how to get organized. After sincere study of each of those books, we made resolutions, fully intending to carry them out.

If there was anything we lacked, it certainly wasn't good intentions, but in time our good intentions turned to desperation. For instance, we intended to start our spring cleaning, but we ended up tearing up much more than we could put back, let alone clean. We intended to can in the summer, so we saved jars of every size, only to let them gather cobwebs and fill with spiders in the garage. We intended to sew all of our children's back-to-school clothes, but only got as far as cutting out the material. We intended to be ready for Christmas by December 1, but on Christmas Eve we found ourselves gluing, painting, wrapping, baking, sewing, and praying that our Visa card would be authorized one more time.

Even in our desperation we kept open minds. We were willing to listen to anyone who could show us another way. We were always tagging after our organized friends. Nancy was our favorite.

Ring...ring...ring...

"Hi, Nancy. What are you doing?"

"Oh, I just finished wallpapering the chicken coop."

"You wallpapered the chicken coop?"

"Yeah, I did it in yellow gingham. The Sheetrock seemed so unfinished."

It wasn't as ridiculous as it sounded, when she explained that a chicken down the street had frozen to death the previous winter. So the following year Nancy's contractor husband had made use of some leftover Sheetrock to insulate their chicken coop, which had led to the yellow gingham. Ridiculous or not, it made us feel even more inferior and desperate.

"My chickens are so happy!"

"I wish I were one of your chickens. I need a nice, clean, quiet, cheerful place to think."

We came to the end of our ropes on June 16, 1977. We were desperately disorganized and utterly disgusted with ourselves. We didn't meet in Nancy's chicken coop but chose a local restaurant instead. We didn't realize the wisdom of that choice until we discovered that by stepping away from the problem, we could see it in a different light. It was impossible for us to think in the confusion and disorder of our homes. There wasn't a place to sit, we couldn't find paper or a pen, the kids were famished, and there was no food in the house. A restaurant was the only answer.

Our kids were used to spontaneous departures. They could throw on their clothes and be out in the station wagon in seventeen seconds. The older ones helped the littlest ones while we changed our headscarves and skillfully applied lipstick.

Our children, ranging in age from twelve years to eighteen months, were pathetic sights. We were oblivious to their twelve mismatched socks, nine missing buttons, six uncombed heads, three runny noses, and one pair of different-colored shoes.

With six children there was never silence. We had learned to be relatively unconcerned about confusion, bickering, teasing, or crying, since out of the batch at least one was always zigging while the others were zagging.

"How many for lunch?" the hostess at the restaurant asked.

We made a quick count. "Nine," we said defensively. The sight of so many children always gave hostesses the willies, as if they were expecting the rest of the chartered bus to come through the door.

We walked to the table like mother ducks, followed by our line of ducklings, all clasping hands. Someone in the group was crying, as usual.

It was one thing to cry loudly in the station wagon, but we demanded more restraint in public places. By the time we got to our table, the crying had turned to uncontrollable screaming. We were devastated by such despicable behavior. It was not characteristic of any one of our six. Hmmm...six...plus two mothers...should be eight for lunch...

Sidetracked again, we accidentally had grabbed the hand of a small boy at the gum machine and kidnapped him. After returning the child to his angry mother, we settled down at our table and began to look at ourselves honestly for the first time.

It was painful to admit our gross inadequacies as homemakers, but we comforted each other after every confession.

"I've actually sprayed dirty socks and undershirts with deodorant and thrown them into the dryer on Tumble Press."

"I use the Air Fluff setting. Have you ever tried to quick-dry undershorts in the microwave? It doesn't work."

"It doesn't work on pantyhose either."

"Sissy, right this minute I've got dirty pots and pans in my oven."

"I can top that: I've filled my oven to capacity and had to stash some stuff in the shower stall."

"Remember when we came home from the zoo and the house had been broken into?"

"Yeah, and the sheriff met you at the car and said somebody's torn up the place."

"Yeah, and I was so embarrassed to tell him that everything was just the way I'd left it."

"I think the reason the burglar didn't take anything was that he couldn't find anything."

"Who could? We live there, and *we* can't even find anything."

We cried and then we started to laugh. Some of our horror stories were actually funny, such as the time one of our husbands drove to work, dragging a king-size fitted bedsheet hooked on the bumper of the car. A pile of dirty laundry had been thrown into the garage to hide it from unexpected company the night before.

What was wrong with us? Were we lazy, or stupid? We thought about people we knew who were organized: our mother, our husbands, and some of our friends who were naturally efficient and tidy. How did they get that way?

It was then that we realized why all the get-organized books hadn't helped us, why our mom had failed to produce perfect homemakers, and why our organized friends, from whom we had begged advice, could only put a Band-Aid on our problems. It was a matter of genetics. They were born organized—usually right on their due date—and we were born sidetracked—with no concept of time. One of us was three weeks late, and the other was three weeks early. It was a relief to see this revelation. If we only had understood it through all those years of struggle and self-condemnation.

We felt like a couple of doctors who had finally made a scientific breakthrough. It was amazing that the answer was so simple.

But it's one thing to discover the reason for a problem, and quite another matter to know what to do about it. So we are handicapped. what did that really mean? It meant that our problem had to be dealt with in a different way, a way that had not yet been thought of.

We decided to meet in the restaurant once a week until we had figured out a way to become organized. In six weeks we created a revolutionary 3x5-card filing system that changed our homes and our lives. At our final meeting, on the sixth week, we delighted in our success and celebrated our victory. The waitress who had served us over those six weeks couldn't help but notice the change.

"What's happened to you two? You look good, you smell

good, your kids have on matching socks. What have you done?"

"We figured out how to get organized."

"Boy, I sure could use some help. You should see my house."

"You're kidding. Your apron's starched, your white work shoes are spotless, your hairnet's in place. You *are* organized."

"Oh, I do okay here at work. I have to or I'd get fired. But at home I'm a slob."

When we realized that we weren't the only two people in the world who suffered from chronic disorganization, we decided to share with others the system that had helped us change. That decision marked the beginning of an organization we now call Sidetracked Home Executives™ (S.H.E.). Our first book, by the same name, explained the system and told the story of our incredible transformation.

As full-time homemakers, we had found little applause. In our slob days, even the dog wouldn't pay attention to us, and the attention we did get was usually negative—rightly so. The way people treated us was a direct reflection of how we felt about ourselves. We didn't wear makeup. We were overweight. On many afternoons we stuffed our fat thighs into our pilled and sprung polyester pantsuits, pressed back our greasy locks with wrinkled bandannas, and headed to the store, thrilled to be out.

Once, a few days before our first meeting in the restaurant, which marked the beginning of our change, we walked past two men sitting on a bench in a shopping mall, women-watching. As we passed by we heard one man say to the other, laughingly, "Hey, there's one for you, Rod." We both looked like dogs and we knew it, but we wondered which one of us they were referring to. We both had our feelings hurt.

We were used to receiving unsolicited pity because of our vocation. Whenever we'd say we were homemakers, instead of getting the appropriate recognition for such a Divine appointment, we found that people would talk very slowly to us so—that—we—could—get—it. At an eruption party— we live only forty miles from the volcano, Mount St. Helens—

an editor of the Pulitzer prize-winning *Longview Daily News* asked one of us in passing, "What do you do?"

"I'm a homemaker."

His dark eyes shifted, severing communication. It was obvious that he was helpless and wished he'd never started the conversation. It was as if he couldn't think of anything to say in response. No doubt, he was thinking, "Should I ask her how to handle ring-around-the-collar or get her solution for stubborn waxy buildup? Maybe she knows what to do when the drain clogs up, and does she really spell relief R-O-L-A-I-D-S?"

Seeing his paralysis and recognizing his deep remorse, it seemed best to respond, "I love being a homemaker."

"Oh, hey, you don't have to apologize for being a homemaker."

"I *did not* apologize for being a homemaker—you apologized for me."

"I did?"

"You did!"

"I *did*, didn't I."

"Yes. You'd have found me more interesting if I'd said I was a fig picker from Fresno and I work in the heat of the day. Then you could have talked down to me about working conditions and the plight of the migrant worker on the fruit circuit."

At social gatherings it wasn't just men who were guilty of looking down on a career in domesticity.

"It's nice to meet you, Peggy."

"Nice to meet you, too, Alexandra."

"Isn't this a mahvelous pahty?"

"Uh huh."

"Do you work, deah?"

"I'm a homemaker."

"Oh. How sweet. DO YOU PLAN TO FINISH SCHOOL and get a real job someday?"

It was as if no one with a brain in her head ever would have chosen to become a homemaker. With us it had been a conscious choice, and we wanted to be professionals in our chosen field.

In an effort to compete with what the world recognized as valuable, we tried all the cutesy titles: "domestic engineer," "president of my address," "virtuous janitor." But our homes were pigpens because of our sidetracked natures and our low self-images.

In our darkest "slob" days we'd see Annette Funicello eating peanut butter on TV and we'd be jealous. She still looked good! Where had we gone wrong? There was a hazy recollection of a time when we were the Annette Funicellos of our high schools. We were popular, we were sought after at dances, and we were CHEERLEADERS! But that was so many years and babies ago. Whom could we blame? At what point did the homecoming princesses become ashamed of their homes? When did the laundry bury the two "Most Likely to Succeeds"? Where was that spark of delight? When had we lost track of ourselves?

As hard as it was for us honestly to compare ourselves with other women our age, we found comfort in an intuitive awareness that our spark had not gone out!

Getting organized rekindled that internal spark of life, giving us a reunion with ourselves. We were able to put the Mickey Mouse Club behind us and take newfound pleasure in being homemakers.

We even changed our response at parties when someone asked, "What do you do?" With a self-righteous dab of Pine Sol behind each ear, we each triumphantly declared: "I am responsible for creating a climate of love, peace, joy, beauty, and order in my home. I am raising future citizens of the United States of America! What do you do?" No other life's work can compare. Even astronauts, attorneys, and doctors paled before us.

2
CONFESSIONS FROM PARADISE

Almost from the first time we shared the system we realized that because it worked, people assumed we were authorities in every area of home management. We found ourselves speaking to large groups and being introduced as efficiency experts. If anything, we were deficiency experts. We had total understanding of the sidetracked nature, and we had learned how to control it and appreciate it—but that was all.

On one occasion we spoke to a group of professional home economists. They were all well-educated women who had devoted their lives to learning and teaching home management. We were flattered to address such a distinguished group of colleagues and relieved that they were gracious enough to accept us and our system, gleaned from experience and desperation, even though we lacked any impressive credentials. With time we earned credibility because our system worked and people changed. But it all seemed to happen too fast.

Shortly after we got organized we were described in our local newspaper as experts in organization, though we'd

only been in control of our lives for six weeks. In that short
time we had changed so completely that it was literally
true—we had gone from pigpen to paradise.

Within two years we had proudly finished our first book
and enjoyed the notoriety we received. Being placed in a
position of authority was flattering at first. People thought
we were responsible for changing their lives when, in
reality, they deserved the credit themselves. That puffed-up
feeling we got from so much overnight attention eventually
led to guilt over several things.

Ring...ring...ring...

"Hello."

"Hi. We ate like animals again tonight, Pam."

"What did your menu plan say?"

"It just said poultry."

"What happened?"

"I don't know. It all happened so fast....I remember
taking a whole chicken out of the oven....It was gorgeous,
Sissy."

"What time was that?"

"I don't know exactly. The kids borrowed the clock
batteries for their Doctor Digital, but I know it was dark
out."

"Dark? Everybody must've been starving."

"Yeah...I remember that."

"Hmmm. We'd better figure this out....Go back to the
last time you saw the chicken intact. What were you
thinking?"

"What was I thinking? Let's see. I was thinking, 'What
will I serve with this splendid bird? There's nothing else on
my menu plan. Where will I go to get the stuff I need to fix
it? What will I use for money when I get there? I can't go to
the store, no money; better set the table and think of
something else to fix.' Oh, yeah, it's starting to come clear
now. I couldn't set the table until the dishwasher shut off,
and while I was waiting I...I...I ate one of his legs, Pam."

"You did?"

"Yeah, and the kids caught me with grease on my face,

and then Danny came through the kitchen to check on dinner and smelled chicken on my breath. . . . The next thing I knew, the bird was gone . . . there was nothing left but a pile of bones. What did you have for dinner?"

"We ate out."

"You ate out last night."

"Yeah, I know . . . we've been eating in restaurants so much lately, we've shot our vacation budget. What's wrong with us? I don't think normal people eat this way."

"Pam, I feel so guilty. Here we are, authorities on organization, and we either eat like animals or tourists."

"I know, and now, with our notoriety, people depend on us for answers."

"Yeah, like the commercial when R. H. Block talks . . . everybody listens!"

"No, they don't . . . it's E.F. Hutton everybody listens to and, anyway, it's H. and R. Block tax consultants."

"Oh, no . . . I sent our receipts to E.F. Hutton."

We were sidetracked by nature and always would be. We could only hope to control our problem by being consciously aware of every move we made. We considered ourselves in nervous remission.

We admitted that we had no talent or love for cleaning, but cooking was another story.

We both loved to cook. We loved to mix things and taste as we'd go. We had a natural flair for seasoning dishes—we got that from Granny—and for coming up with entire dinners from barren pantries. We soaked up the compliments that followed a tasty meal, whether it was a crisis casserole or a flash-in-the-pan entree (recipes start page 176). But all our meals were started too late and ended with that feeling of "Is that all there is?"

If we both loved to cook and we had a natural talent for it, then why were most of our dinners prepared in frustration and served with guilt? Why did we eat the way we did?

We knew we wanted our meals to be well planned, with lots of variety, and served at a regular time. We wanted our kitchens to be gathering places for our families, filled with delicious food and wonderful memories. We loved the aroma of coffee brewing and bread that had nearly finished baking. When invited to someone's home for dinner, we admired the fine linens, china, and crystal that were elegantly set upon the dining room table, assuring the hungry guests that a scrumptious meal was about to be served.

In our disorganized days, our dining tables usually were covered with everything but food and fineries. Somehow they had become the stopping places for unanswered mail, unfolded laundry, craft projects of every kind, children's school papers, and a portable TV set. We had never used the china we'd collected for years. It remained stacked in the highest cupboard, except for the six matching pieces cleverly displayed in our hutches. The silver, tarnished and abandoned, lay waiting for Mom to come and shine it. Polishing silver had been one of the things we crossed off our lists when we first got organized. We just weren't ready to get to it. Back in our slob days, when beds weren't made and everyday dishes were piled high in the sink, who could think about polishing silver?

Our kitchen inventories were evidence of our addiction to garage sales: a popcorn popper marked "works good" (it lied), an electric frying pan with a lazy thermostat, a Sno-Kone machine, Popsicle molds, and a Crock-Pot with the "do not submerge" feature. The list looked like an impulse-buyer's guide. Garage sales were just the place to buy secondhand impulse-ware.

Our teapots were testimony to our sidetracked personalities and showed the scars of abuse, exposure, and dehydration. Our plates were chipped, our pans were warped, our copper was green, our spoons were bent, our lids were missing, and the red writing had long since disappeared from our measuring cups. Our kitchen knives were dull, and our appliances were crippled with neglect and age.

"Sissy, would you whip that pint of cream for the strawberries?"

"Yeah. Where's the other beater?"

"It's in the drawer, but don't ever use it. You can't use them both at the same time."

"Why?"

"Well, I ran a spoon through them once when it was on 'High Whip,' and ever since that day, if you use them together, they click and spray stuff all over the kitchen."

"Pam, you've gotta get a new mixer or get this one fixed."

"Hey, you should talk. What about your blender? It goes straight from one to ten, and you've got tape over number four. What happens, Peggy, when you punch number four?"

"I don't want to talk about it."

"Come on, Sissy. What happens?"

"Well...uh..."

"Come on. What does it *say* will happen?"

"It says 'Chop.'"

"And...?"

"Well, the whole plastic container leaves the machine. If NASA could only get hold of the ejection principle of that blender...!"

"Peggy, just use the one beater and beat it twice as long as the recipe says. Okay?"

"Okay!"

We never made complete meals, just as we had never finished quilts or paintings or our vacuuming. We prided ourselves on never sending our families to bed hungry, though. They'd be full, but usually of just one food. The idea of serving a balanced diet, with a main dish, vegetable, carbohydrate, salad, dessert, and beverage, was an advanced concept for us. It was not only advanced, it was so nutritionally sound that it was downright intimidating (see boring list of "Foods for Everyday," pp. 156–157). Take dessert, for instance. Dessert, that special touch, that final addition to a wonderful meal. Ha! We were lucky to have had a meal.

"Mom, how come at Matthew's house they always have dessert?"

"I don't know. They must not care about their teeth."

"No, Matthew's dad is a dentist."

"Humph. Dessert? What did they have when you stayed there?"

"I don't know what they called it, but it was on fire for a while."

"Humph."

"Matthew's mom is a really good cook!"

"Humph. I'll bet she's fat."

"No, she's not. She's real little."

"Jeff, eat your dinner, and then you can have graham crackers and you can open a bag of chocolate chips."

"All right!!!"

"Jeff?"

"Yeah?"

"You don't need to tell Matthew or his mother what you had for dessert. We have the freedom to conceal what we eat in the privacy of our own home. It's an American right, according to our Constitution."

We relied totally on Flintstones to provide our children with the vitamins and minerals their little bodies craved. We knew that most cold cereals had less nutritional value than the boxes they came in, but in the name of convenience, that's what our kids ate.

Our business commitments took us outside of our homes, and we were lured into the world of convenience foods. Fast-food restaurants took the place of home-cooked meals.

Once again, we'd had it. It was true that our kitchens were clean, but they were not organized. Dishes were no longer piled in the oven, stashed in the shower stall, or left on the dining room table. We no longer drank out of jelly jars or bowls, or wrecked important papers by accidentally setting them down in puddles on our kitchen counters. We definitely had mastered the routine of dishwashing, and we had won the battle of our refrigerators, which in the past were so full of bacterial life that they could almost walk from room to room. Our kitchen floors shone—open-heart surgery could have been performed on them—our windows glistened, our ovens gleamed, and our light fixtures sparkled, reflecting the progress we had made. But in all that cleanliness we had to face the fact that we were still disorganized.

We were so ashamed. We were guilty of hypocrisy! We hadn't intentionally snowed the public in our first book by saying, "...skip the kitchen for now. Once you've organized the rest of your house, you'll have confidence and experience and you'll automatically know what to do!" Ha. We had waited three years for that automatic knowledge to come. How could we have thought that anything in the area of organization would come automatically? We went on to say in the book, "...we won't try to give you any arbitrary rules"—because there were no rules—"...we suggest working logically"—Sidetracked Home Executives™ never work logically—"taking time to think"—they never take time to think, either—"...and contacting a local county extension agent for advice." Who?

The menu plan in our first book was primitive, but somehow it sparked creativity in women who were born organized. In letters, they marveled at how wonderfully the system worked in the kitchen and at mealtimes. We read the letters in amazement and curiosity. But other women wrote in desperation, "Help! I've cleaned my entire house, but I don't quite understand what to do with my kitchen." It seemed shallow to send a form letter advising, "Reread the last paragraph on page 103 of Chapter Five and good luck!" We were as desperate about our kitchens as anyone else.

We decided that there was no point in feeling guilty. We had done the best we could with what we had known at the time. We both knew that guilt wouldn't help change the problem. It was only a sign that we were off the track and out of control. Once a person makes the decision to change, she/he no longer needs the guilty signal. That would be like sitting at a red light after it had turned green.

We remembered how overwhelming the housework had seemed on June 16, 1977, the day we decided to change. Now, five years later, we realize that what we have accomplished is incredible, and to feel guilty for what we hadn't yet done was a waste of time and energy. We forgive ourselves for our shortcomings and look at the whole problem the way you do when you've got a lousy haircut. You work with it until it grows out.

3

NEAT V. EAT

Of all the rooms in the house, the kitchen was most important to us. Our families deserved to be served tempting, nutritious food, and we deserved to have efficient, cheerful kitchens to work in.

We were ready to change our old ways, but we knew that with any attempt to improve, our motive had to be right. If we conquered the kitchen just so that we could get compliments, it wouldn't work. If we did it just so we could have an intelligent response to questions from other Sidetracked Home Executives,™ that would be wrong. We had to make the effort for ourselves and our families.

We coaxed ourselves into an uncharted area—the kitchen—knowing we would be guided by a wisdom greater than our own. We found our work became coupled with a sense of love. We knew the result would be cheerful, efficient kitchens just like the one our mom had.

But before we could start any kitchen system, we needed to know what had stopped us from incorporating that room into our original plan. Whenever we talked about our dilemma, we found ourselves spouting a bunch of extenuating circumstances. We were experts at making excuses. Over the years we realized that the excuses helped us feel better. When things weren't the way we wanted them to be, an excuse seemed easier to use than the stove.

"Creative people are messy!" we said defensively, to offset the fact that there wasn't a chair to sit on or a place to set a cup of coffee. Excuses were necessary for our emotional health before we were ready to challenge our problem. Excuses kept us from twitching, stuttering, and possibly being committed to a mental institution. An excuse is like putting a wig over a bad haircut. But it was very disconcerting to discover that even after we had got organized, old Mr. Excuse once again had crept into our kitchens with his lengthy list:

1. Miss Cratsberry never taught me.
2. I just cleaned up from the last meal.
3. It's too hot to cook.
4. The refrigerator light is out.
5. I'm out of eggs.
6. I can't find a bowl.
7. I feel like a short-order cook.
8. I've been in the kitchen all day.
9. The sink's stopped up.
10. When I do cook a good meal, nobody comes when I call.
11. My kitchen's too small.
12. My kitchen was designed by a man who never fixed a meal in his life.
13. I don't have the right equipment.
14. I need a microwave.
15. I need a Cuisinart.
16. I'm on a diet.
17. The kids are finicky eaters.
18. I'm tired of cooking the same old things.
19. Nobody likes what I cook.
20. My counter's too high.
21. My counter's too low.

In the last three years our list of excuses had changed. We had eliminated some of our troublesome circumstances, but new problems, just as valid as the old, had taken their place. When it wasn't too hot to cook, it was too cold. We'd replace the refrigerator light only to have the thermostat go out. We'd unplug the sink at just about the time the dishwasher would back up. Finally we realized that we could go another three years, relying on new excuses to justify our predicament, but if we wanted improvement, the excuses would have to go.

We were ready to take action. We just didn't know where to start.

Should we first reorganize, starting with the pantry, cupboards, and drawers? Should we clean and defrost the freezer; buy a microwave oven, a wok, a pastry-maker; or should we buy a set of matching silverware first?

We wondered if the problem stemmed from having too many pans and not enough lids, or from too many cookbooks and a lousy menu plan.

Should we take gourmet-cooking lessons, or should we go through all of our old magazines for new recipes to try?

Should we remodel our kitchens or reevaluate our eating habits?

Should we get out our sewing machines and make Donna Reed aprons, or should we buy hairnets, white shoes, and support stockings, like cafeteria workers?

Should we plant a garden and get a couple of cows and some chickens, or should we go to the Can Can and buy cases of fruits and vegetables?

We were confused, but we remembered how enslaved we had been a few years ago with just the dishes, laundry, and daily clutter. Back then we wished we could have moved out of our pigpens into brand new homes, with all new stuff and a built-in efficiency expert who would tell us exactly where to put everything and where to begin each day's work.

In our pigpen days when we decided to change, we didn't have anyone to tell us where to start. All the homemaking books we had read were written by authors who would never have believed the extent of the mess we were in. We had to pick a starting place, knowing that if it was the wrong one, at least we had started somewhere, and that would be better than just thinking or talking about it.

Now, with our kitchens, it was time to stop talking and start organizing. Logically, we could rule out several alternatives: the cow, the chickens, and the hairnets were out. Instead of sewing them, we bought Donna Reed aprons; it was winter, so the garden could wait; we couldn't afford to remodel; and the cannery was closed for the season. The remaining choices were to concentrate on cooking lessons, come up with a menu system, do an equipment inventory, or totally reorganize the freezer, pantry, cupboards, and drawers.

We had just returned from Wok-King—a Chinese restaurant—when it was obvious we should rule out the cooking classes.

"What's the matter, Sissy?"

"Oh, nothing. I've got pork in my teeth."

"Good lunch, huh?"

"Yeah."

"Where's your doggy bag?"

"Oh, shoot. I left it in the restroom."

"That's better than leaving it in the car. Last summer I left a couple of crab legs in the station wagon, and every cat in the neighborhood was in the driveway."

"Whatever happened to that car? Did you ever get the smell out?"

"Nope. We sold it to a guy at the beach."

"You wanna take a class in Chinese cooking over at the college with me?"

"Oh, I don't know. Who teaches it this quarter?"

"Mel Davis."

"Spare me. Has he been to China?"

"No, but he fought in the Korean conflict and he came back loaded with recipes."

"Do the Chinese cook the same as the Koreans do?"

"I don't know. Just sign up with me."

"Doesn't Mel Davis teach painting on velvet?"

"Yeah. I'm telling you, Sissy. He's really been everywhere. He even spent some time in Mexico."

"Yeah, I know. I've seen his bumper stickers."

"Don't judge a man's cooking ability by his bumper stickers. Do you want to go with me or not?"

"No!"

"No?"

"No. We've gotta be able to cook the basics on a regular basis before we move into international cooking."

It was true. How could we have the nerve to bring home Chinese recipes when we weren't even taking the time to make Jell-O? The cooking classes would be postponed.

Now we were torn. Was it more important to know what we were going to cook or to have a perfectly organized, well-equipped kitchen to cook in?

Persuaded by a single factor—HUNGER—and knowing how easily we could improvise with equipment, we both agreed that meals should come before inventory and organization. We felt it would be ridiculous to spend money on a pastry-maker when we were out of flour. Why reorganize the pantry and cupboards when they were empty? Why remodel the kitchen when everybody ate in the family room?

The hunger factor convinced us that we needed a good menu plan, more comprehensive than just one 3x5 card with a list of seven main dishes. We wanted complete menus with side dishes, vegetables, and desserts. We wanted to have enough menus in advance so that we could choose from a variety of combinations without having to think. We wanted to spend less time on weekly menu-planning by having already figured out those wonderful combinations.

We wanted our menu system to speed up the whole process of planning the food, making the grocery list, shopping the ads, and looking up recipe ingredients. Our system would, of course, eliminate writing and rewriting lists. We would start, as we had with organizing housework, with one master list. Then we would transfer everything on the

list to 3x5 cards. We would file the cards in categories in
our card-file kits and choose and rotate them so that our
families would enjoy variety. We were ready to start, and it
was a great feeling.

4

SIDETRACKERS BEWARE

WARNING: The menu system contained in this book is an advanced concept and may be hazardous to your mental health. Use as directed AFTER the rest of your house is under control.

By the time we created our 3x5 menu system, our houses had been clean and free of clutter for more than three years. We were ready to move into the wonderful world of organized food preparation. We suggest that if your house is a mess, you tackle it first by using our basic household card-file system. It's explained in detail, with charts and illustrations, in our first book, *Sidetracked Home Executives.*™ If you try to improve both areas at the same time, you will exceed the recommended dosage of order. Such an overdose of organization may result in harmful, if not fatal, side effects: loss of interest, fatigue, irritability, restlessness, permanent weight gain, resentment, and anger.

We know how you are if you're one of us. You'll get so excited at the thought of order in your kitchen and freedom from meal-planning that you'll announce to the family, "Things are gonna change around here. From now on we eat promptly at five."

Then you'll buy a bunch of 3x5 cards and start jotting down menus at random. As you skid on a glob of Play-Doh on the kitchen floor, you'll start a cleaning list while you're thinking of it: "Wash kitchen floor."

You'll vow to change the family's eating habits as you wildly load up a grocery cart with new variety. You'll be almost driven—for about four days. Then, confused and exhausted, and wincing in pain from the Lego caught between your second and third toes, you'll flop into a chair, burnt out.

If we have described you and the way you behave when you're given a new idea, consider yourself a sidetracker. It's nothing to be ashamed of. We sidetrackers are delightful people, actually. It's just that we've never quite come home from the fair.

We're a little bit afraid to tell you to put down this book and go to the nearest bookstore and get our first book. We're afraid, if you're like us, that you'll get on the freeway and forget where you're going. Or you'll make it to the shopping mall and end up trying on bathing suits or having your ears pierced. That's why we've decided to give you a concentrated summary of our household system right here. Obviously we're only going to go over the main points, but we hope we can give you a basic knowledge of the way it works.

We began with an Activity List. It was the basis for our system and the tool for organizing our houses and our lives. It was a room-by-room master list of every household job. It also listed any family-related jobs or errands, plus personal things, that needed to be done. It included everything from filling the dishwasher to reading stories to our children; waxing floors to painting our nails. The list in its entirety is in our first book, *Sidetracked Home Executives.*™

We took each item on our list and decided how often it should be done: daily, weekly, monthly, yearly, etc. Then we put a time estimate on each activity—how long we thought it took us to finish a job. We knew we needed to be aware of time, because losing time—sometimes months and years—is a problem typical of sidetrackers.

We also decided whether a job could be delegated to a husband or child, and whether it was a Mini-Job. A Mini-Job is any project that takes ten minutes or less to complete. We emphasized Mini-Jobs on the Activity List because, if you're sidetracked by nature, you can go through the day unaware of what you could have done with small blocks of time.

Our next step was to draw up a Basic Week Plan. This was a flexible guide to help us spread our work and activities through the week. We set up a free day for ourselves, free from housework, elaborate cooking, and errands. It was our reward for being so well organized. Then we included: a moderate-cleaning day; a quiet day, for paying bills, balancing the checkbook, clipping grocery coupons, writing letters, and tying up loose ends; a grocery shopping day; a heavy-cleaning day; a family day; and Sunday, which we keep free.

We found the plan could be varied for women with jobs outside their homes, and later adopted the modified schedule ourselves.

The next step in the system was transferring the Activity List to color-coded 3x5 cards. For example, we used *yellow* cards for all daily jobs, one job to a card. *Blue* cards were for all weekly jobs. *White* cards were for monthly and seasonal jobs. *Pink* cards were for all personal things, the things we loved to do, and jobs or errands outside the home.

On each card we wrote the job's title, whether it could be delegated, a description of the job, its estimated time limit, whether or not it was a Mini-Job, and its frequency.

When we started our system we needed cards for everything, because we wouldn't do a job if we didn't have a card for it. But now that we've been on the system for so long, we've found that many jobs have become automatic, and we've been able to throw away many of our original cards. Probably you'll start your own file with fewer 3x5s than ours had, because we were the ultimate slobs.

Next in our setup came the one through thirty-one dividers, which became our rotating monthly "calendar" in the file box. We started with the divider numbered with the current date, then filed the rest of the dividers, in order, behind it. Each night we rotated the date just ended to the back of the numbers, so the current date was always at the front of the box.

By then we were ready to start filing. We made four piles of cards, separated by color, and filed individual cards from each pile (pink, yellow, blue, and white) in front of its appropriate day, date, and month.

We filed the daily, weekly, and monthly cards according to our Basic Week Plan, depending on whether the job fit into our moderate-cleaning, heavy-cleaning, quiet, grocery shopping, family, or free day.

In the first few weeks of using our system, we tried desperately to do every card in our file at the appointed time. We made it through the daily and personal cards without much trouble, but some of the weekly and monthly jobs—like waxing floors and washing windows—were real dogs.

Through trial and error and lots of guilt, we came up with a way to give the system flexibility and freedom, and still prevent jobs from piling up beyond our ability to cope. We called the system's fail-safe device "File It and Forget It." We permitted ourselves to skip a job twice before it had to become a priority item.

We found that sometimes it was necessary and possible to skip a whole day or a week of cards. When an old friend came to town on what should have been our heavy-cleaning day, when we went on vacation or when we canned pears for a week, we just skipped all the cards and filed them for when we would be back to normal. Why? We wanted our get-organized system to reflect our philosophy of life: to put people, and our love for them, before vacuum cleaners and dishcloths.

We loved the system. We had never felt so well organized or so much in control of our lives. Our houses were clean, our families were happy, and we had time for ourselves.

As the months passed we grew with the system, expanding it into every area of homemaking except meal-planning and kitchen organization. We knew it could be applied there, too, but we weren't sure how.

5

THE BEST LAID PLANS ARE FOR THE BIRDS

Planning is one of the hardest things for a sidetracker to do. It goes against our nature. It takes too long. We would reason, "Why plan it when we could be doing it?" So we'd dive into everything, expecting automatic direction. But since there is no such thing as automatic direction for the sidetracked person, we'd find ourselves in the middle of several consuming projects all at the same time.

Always optimistic, we had no concept of our own limitations until it was too late. The sequence of events was always the same. Step one was to get the idea, which usually came from someone else—an enchanting talk-show guest with a book on "How To Do It for Less Than $25," or a clever advertisement in a magazine, outlining the ten simple steps to remodeling your kitchen. We also were suckers for the Diet of the Stars weight-loss program, dazzled by the "before" and "after" pictures of celebrities we'd never heard of. But most often the inspiration for a special project would come with the news of impending houseguests or an upcoming party. We would picture everything being perfect. Then we'd make a list of what to do to get it that way.

THINGS TO DO

1. Wallpaper the guest room.
2. Paint the living room.
3. Refinish the picnic table.
4. Make a quilt to match the wallpaper in the guest room.
5. Steam-clean the carpets.

The list was unreasonable but, in our blind optimism, we wouldn't realize it until the doorbell rang. Often we found ourselves in more of a mess than we would have been in if we hadn't done anything. Apologizing for half-papered walls and damp carpeting, we'd warn guests to step around the quilt frame and walk on the drop cloth, and then we'd excuse ourselves and dash to the store for something quick to serve for dinner.

It wouldn't be anything like we'd pictured it.

Besides planning and following through, organized people always read instructions. The reading not only saves time, it also tells a person how much time is necessary to do the project. Sidetracked people hate to read instructions, partly because of the time it takes, but mostly because after we take the time to read the manual, we're completely out of the mood.

"In an inconspicuous area of the room, remove several sample carpet fibers for testing their colorfastness. If after twenty-four hours the test fibers reveal an alteration in color or a deterioration in structure, we cannot be responsible for your use of our product."

Since risk has never been a part of our concern, it always seemed better just to clean the carpet and, if it turned another color, to welcome the change.

Aside from our dislike of planning, we didn't want to become like Ordell, who cannot make a move without a written plan. She would routinely organize every aspect of her life, then flaunt her plan.

"Ordell, do you plan menus?"

"Yes, I do! I take two hours every Tuesday and I jot down the things I need for the week. I consult the advertised specials in the newspaper for the four grocery stories I patronize. I color-code my leftovers, I organize my coupons, I rotate my perishables, and I take back my bottles. I compile seven menus, which are classified by calorie content and geared to the productive activity scale of each member of the family on any given day. I—"

"Ordell?"

"I'm here."

"Do you have that written down anywhere?"

"Frankly, I've never found it necessary."

We all know someone like Ordell. You can spot her in any grocery store. She's overcoordinated with matching purse, shoes, earrings, necklace, bracelet, lipstick, and nail polish, toes included. She has her list in one hand, a three-fingered manual calculator—the plastic kind that clicks—in the other, and a map of the store decoupaged on pressboard, specifically designed to fit snugly in the baby seat of her grocery cart.

The best time to find her is on any weekday morning when the store opens, or especially on Saturday around 10 A.M., after her standing hair appointment, so to speak. The only time you'd see a Sidetracked Home Executive™ at a grocery store first thing in the morning would be because she needed milk for cereal, and if you looked closely, you'd see her nightgown wadded up inside her jeans. (Note: You'll never see the Ordells of the world at a checkout counter after 4 P.M.)

After 4 P.M. the Sidetracked Home Executive™ comes out of her house and heads for the store, with the same confused look on her face as a person coming out of a dark, air-conditioned theater after a summer matinee. She's trailed by several hungry children. She wears a wig, the same one she got for entry into the Pork-of-the-Month Club. The choice of wigs came after signing up, and the pork followed.

Unfortunately, to make the club pay off, she had to consume an incredible amount of pork each month. Consequently, she's a few pounds overweight. Sidetracked people should never sign up for anything of- or by-the-month. In fact, sidetracked people should never sign up for anything. The wig will be tied down and held securely with a colorful scarf that will match absolutely nothing. It actually might violently conflict with the rest of the outfit. Her nails will show evidence of carelessness and abandon. Toenails will almost never be polished, because they are so far away from the brain that they are rarely thought of. If they are painted, of course, they too will match nothing.

Her purse resembles a duffel bag, and her wallet and checkbook may or may not be in it. What will be in it, and this is universal, will be candy and gum wrappers of every kind; credit card receipts from gas station and restaurant purchases; ticket stubs; pennies; a couple of insurance company pens that don't write; an emery board without emery powder; a claim ticket from the dry cleaners for clothes already picked up and signed for, because the claim ticket couldn't be found; several smooshed Junior Mints and/or Milk Duds; business cards from the home show; bobby pins; one earring; a pretty rock; several illegible bank deposit slips; sand; and miscellaneous pocket fuzz.

The Sidetracked Home Executive's™ shopping cart will be crammed full of convenience foods high in calories but easy to throw at the kids to put them on hold while she scrounges up a real dinner. She won't be able to find her car in the parking lot, and she won't be wearing a watch. She'll be coming out of the store when the Ordells of the world are ready to change into long dresses for the evening.

We know her so well because we are her sisters. We wish we had a dollar for every time we started grocery shopping at 5 P.M. for that night's dinner. It's taken us three years to get organized in the kitchen, and the key to it has been learning to plan. We were always afraid that planning would stifle our creativity, but what can appear to be a prison—"I've gotta sit down and plan this out"—turns out to be freedom. After all, unless you're Marvin Hamlisch's

ORDELL DAILY—BORN ORGANIZED

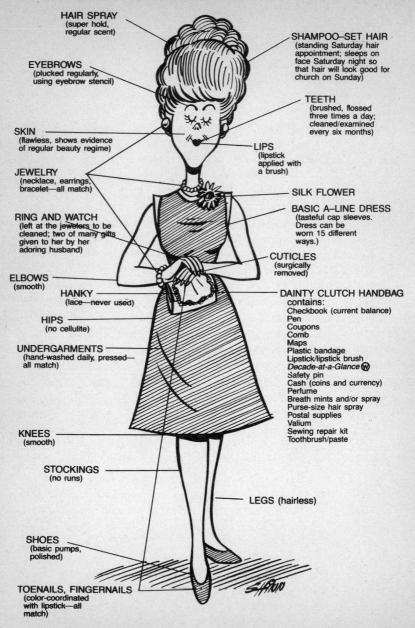

HAIR SPRAY
(super hold, regular scent)

SHAMPOO—SET HAIR
(standing Saturday hair appointment; sleeps on face Saturday night so that hair will look good for church on Sunday)

EYEBROWS
(plucked regularly, using eyebrow stencil)

TEETH
(brushed, flossed three times a day; cleaned/examined every six months)

SKIN
(flawless, shows evidence of regular beauty regime)

LIPS
(lipstick applied with a brush)

JEWELRY
(necklace, earrings, bracelet—all match)

SILK FLOWER

RING AND WATCH
(left at the jewelers to be cleaned; two of many gifts given to her by her adoring husband)

BASIC A–LINE DRESS
(tasteful cap sleeves. Dress can be worn 15 different ways.)

CUTICLES
(surgically removed)

ELBOWS
(smooth)

HANKY
(lace—never used)

DAINTY CLUTCH HANDBAG
contains:
Checkbook (current balance)
Pen
Coupons
Comb
Maps
Plastic bandage
Lipstick/lipstick brush
Decade-at-a-Glance Ⓦ
Safety pin
Cash (coins and currency)
Perfume
Breath mints and/or spray
Purse-size hair spray
Postal supplies
Valium
Sewing repair kit
Toothbrush/paste

HIPS
(no cellulite)

UNDERGARMENTS
(hand-washed daily, pressed—all match)

KNEES
(smooth)

STOCKINGS
(no runs)

LEGS (hairless)

SHOES
(basic pumps, polished)

TOENAILS, FINGERNAILS
(color-coordinated with lipstick—all match)

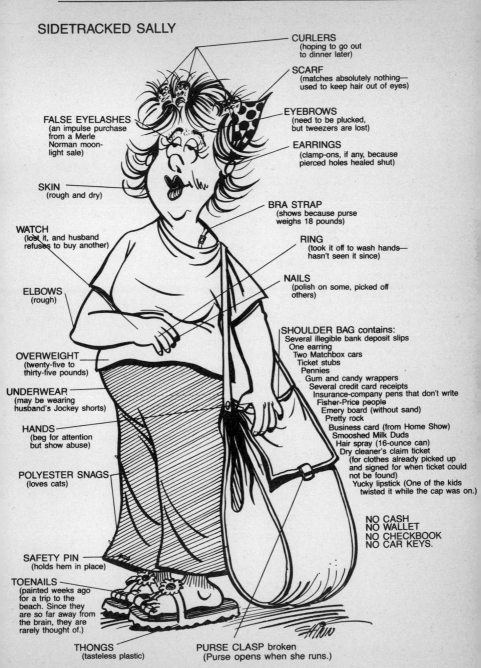

SIDETRACKED SALLY

CURLERS
(hoping to go out
to dinner later)

SCARF
(matches absolutely nothing—
used to keep hair out of eyes)

FALSE EYELASHES
(an impulse purchase
from a Merle
Norman moon-
light sale)

EYEBROWS
(need to be plucked,
but tweezers are lost)

EARRINGS
(clamp-ons, if any, because
pierced holes healed shut)

SKIN
(rough and dry)

BRA STRAP
(shows because purse
weighs 18 pounds)

WATCH
(lost it, and husband
refuses to buy another)

RING
(took it off to wash hands—
hasn't seen it since)

NAILS
(polish on some, picked off
others)

ELBOWS
(rough)

SHOULDER BAG contains:
Several illegible bank deposit slips
One earring
Two Matchbox cars
Ticket stubs
Pennies
Gum and candy wrappers
Several credit card receipts
Insurance-company pens that don't write
Fisher-Price people
Emery board (without sand)
Pretty rock
Business card (from Home Show)
Smooshed Milk Duds
Hair spray (16-ounce can)
Dry cleaner's claim ticket
(for clothes already picked up
and signed for when ticket could
not be found)
Yucky lipstick (One of the kids
twisted it while the cap was on.)

OVERWEIGHT
(twenty-five to
thirty-five pounds)

UNDERWEAR
(may be wearing
husband's Jockey shorts)

HANDS
(beg for attention
but show abuse)

POLYESTER SNAGS
(loves cats)

NO CASH
NO WALLET
NO CHECKBOOK
NO CAR KEYS.

SAFETY PIN
(holds hem in place)

TOENAILS
(painted weeks ago
for a trip to the
beach. Since they
are so far away from
the brain, they are
rarely thought of.)

THONGS
(tasteless plastic)

PURSE CLASP broken
(Purse opens when she runs.)

mother, you can't see *A Chorus Line* on the spur of the moment without tickets. Life requires a certain degree of planning, and a person with the gift of spontaneity and flexibility will only add color to the plans.

"Hey, I've got tickets to see *Chorus Line*. How about going to the theater in a hot-air balloon?"

We'll never lose our gift. But so many times it had become a fantasy: "Hey, I sure wish I'd got tickets to *A Chorus Line*. We had a chance to go in a hot-air balloon."

The main part of planning is decision-making, another part of our nature that is semifunctional. When it comes to deciding anything, we'd rather not. Deciding what our families would eat at the next meal was hard enough; to decide what to serve for the next seven days was so far beyond us, we made jokes about it.

Despite the fact that we hate the thought of planning, there had been many occasions when we'd forced ourselves to sit down and figure things out, and we had actually enjoyed it. The bad part was that the plans were short-term, and soon we'd had to sit back down and plan some more. It was the repetition that we detested. It reminded us of Ordell. She spent two hours every Tuesday, fifty-two Tuesdays a year, one hundred four hours annually, planning menus. It hit us that we wouldn't hate menu-planning if we had to do it only once. If we spent two hours a day, not counting weekends, and wrote down as many menu combinations as we could think of in two weeks, we would have spent twenty hours doing it, or one fifth the time Ordell spent, not counting the time it took for her to make her maps and monitor her family's activity-dependent calorie intake.

We figured with just two weeks of planning, we'd be eighty-four hours ahead of Ordell and we'd never have to think again.

PLAN YOUR WORK AND EAT YOUR PLAN

Our lives have improved so much since we discovered the 3x5 card. Our motto is "We change lives with 3x5s." We know that our level of peace, harmony, beauty, love, and power is in direct proportion to how much time we spend with our cards.

When we created the system for housework, we started by drawing up a master activity list. It was only natural to start our new kitchen system with lists, too, one for planning meals and one (to be explained in Chapter Eight) for maintenance.

We knew we didn't want to have to sit down weekly and decide on seven menus for the coming week, so we took the next logical approach. We planned menus to last a year. We realize that sounds incredible, but sidetracked people are incredible, and once a sidetracked person gets on the right track, there is no stopping her or him.

Can you picture this? It's the day the grocery ads come out in the newspaper. You reach for a small file box and, considering what's on sale, you pull out seven absolutely delicious-sounding menu cards that use the foods that are the best buys. On a copy of your master grocery list, you mark off the necessary items. In fifteen minutes you're ready to head to the store to buy just exactly what you need for the next week. You post seven cards on a calico bulletin board in your bright and cheery kitchen. Everyone can mull over the exciting meals he or she will eat in the coming week. Your husband is impressed. You are impressed. What a change from the frozen dinners and the trail from your front door to McDonald's.

To set up this system for planning menus and shopping for food, and a system for maintaining organized kitchen cupboards and drawers, refrigerator and freezer, you will need these supplies:

    1 recipe file box
    1 package of 1-31 dividers
    1 package of ABC dividers
    1 package of rainbow 3x5 cards (blue, yellow, pink) (100)
    1 package of white 3x5 cards (100)
   15 blank dividers

Through the next three chapters as we explain how to set up the system, you will see how to use each of the above. We recommend that you read all three chapters through before you fill anything out. Then come back to this chapter to begin your six-week program.

First Week (first two weeks if you have a job outside your home*)

Make a list of all your family's favorite main dishes. Here is a Menu-Planning Sheet; more are provided on pp. 172–173. They have been divided into six categories: beef, poultry, pork, seafood, lamb, and specialties. In our families, "specialties" include Swedish meatballs, spaghetti, pizza, navy bean soup, etc. Notice that we have separated the menu-

---

*If you have any babies two years old or younger, consider it the same as having a job outside your home.

Menu-Planning Sheet

Beef Main Dish	S/S Side	S/S Vegetables	S/S Desserts	Extras	Salads	F/W Side	F/W Vegetables	F/W Desserts

planning sheets into spring/summer (S/S) and fall/winter (F/W).

In making the list, it will help greatly to have a family council meeting and brainstorm. Get out all of your favorite cookbooks and your recipe file, if you have one. This will help everyone think of his or her favorite foods.

While you are working on the menu-planning sheets, start filling out a master grocery list. (See an example of ours on page 169.) The grocery list won't be complete until you have filled out all the planning sheets, because you'll keep adding new items as you think of them.

We started our master grocery list by using a blank sheet of notebook paper and writing down eleven main categories: meat, canned goods, dairy products, frozen foods, spices and herbs, convenience foods, bakery products, staples, produce, beverages, and general merchandise. We also wrote down the places in which to buy specialty items. If you shop in only one supermarket, arrange your grocery list to correspond to the layout of the store.

When you think of a main dish jot it on the menu-planning sheets. If there is a recipe for it, write down whether it's in a favorite cookbook or in your own recipe file. Refer to the recipe and record all the ingredients that should be added to the master grocery list. Suppose the main dish were meatloaf. You would write *meatloaf* on your menu-planning sheet under the category of "specialty." On the master grocery list you would jot down hamburger, eggs, bread crumbs, salt, pepper, garlic, onions, and ketchup in their appropriate categories.

Eventually, when the menu-planning sheets are completed, you'll have a huge grocery list with everything you would ever need to prepare all of your family's favorite foods. It's a good idea to leave room on the list in each category for new items you'll want to try. You'll also need a section of blank spaces for write-ins. When your master grocery list is finished, have fifty-two copies photocopied for a year's supply. Having your own personal grocery list duplicated is an excellent time-saving tool for future shopping.

Next, after your list of main dishes, decide on the accompaniments you'll want to serve. In the Appendix you'll find five separate pages (164–168) for planning. They are headed Side Dishes (potatoes, rice, noodles, etc.), Vegetables, Desserts, Extras, and Salads.

Again using your family, cookbooks, and recipe file, think of every possible accompaniment food in each category and write it down. Remember, whenever you choose a food from a cookbook recipe, write the recipe's page number and the initials of the cookbook on the planning sheet in the space marked "Recipe Source." If the food comes from your own recipe file, make that notation. You will end up with five pages of accompaniments, which will be mixed and matched (the second week) into delicious combinations with the main dishes already listed on your menu-planning sheets.

At this point we recommend that you stop temporarily. This is enough of a project for one week. We know how easy it is to get involved in a project to the exclusion of everyone and everything else in your life. Chances are, if you've gone this far, there are other household tasks that need your attention.

If you followed our filing system for organizing your home, you know how overwhelming all those cards can be. If there is anything we can't say often enough, it's be easy on yourself. Do this gradually.

Second Week (Remember to double the time if you have a job outside your home.)

In the second week you will be planning actual menus. We suggest that you skip lunch all this week and use that time to work on filling out your menu-planning sheets with accompaniment lists. It's so simple but true that you can think up better food combinations when you're hungry. We both discovered that after we'd eaten a meal and tried to go back to work on the menu-planning sheets. Our full stomachs killed the creativity we'd had before the meal.

Before you start filling out the menu-planning sheets, be

sure you have completed all of your accompaniment lists. It's important to start with as many choices as you can think of. We also suggest that you have a partner. We got together at this point and helped each other with variety and ideas. It's important that your partner have tastes similar to yours. Your spouse could be the perfect partner. (See page 172 for an example of one of our completed Menu-Planning Sheets.)

Now go down the main dish column of the menu-planning sheets, with your list of side dishes at hand, and distribute the side dishes where they would taste best. Steak and baked potatoes, for instance, is an excellent combination, whereas steak with macaroni and cheese is only found on the excursion flight from Cleveland to Pittsburgh.

After you've completely filled out the side dish column on the menu-planning sheets, move on to the list of vegetables, then desserts, extras, and salads. As you fill out the planning sheets with the five pages of accompaniments, be sure to write cookbook initials and page numbers on it, just as you did with the main dishes. You will already have written them on your original lists.

Remember to keep adding to your master grocery list through all of the accompaniment lists. If you're like us, you don't much like to make decisions and you may find yourself thinking too hard about whether you are putting down the right vegetable, side dish, or whatever. It's very important to note that you will have *two more chances* to change what you initially wrote: once when you write out the menu cards, and again when it's time to fix the meal. For now, don't worry; just keep filling out the menu-planning sheets.

It will take you about a week if you work an entire hour every day (don't forget to skip lunch) to complete your menu-planning sheets. When we filled out ours, we did them for the entire year. If you want to work on just the current season, and you know yourself well enough to be sure that later you will work on the other half of the year, that's fine. We didn't trust ourselves to do just half. It really depends on how sidetracked you are.

It's a good idea to keep what you're doing a secret, because you're going to spend several weeks on this. If your family knows what you are doing, they might start expecting something they aren't going to get yet. It's reasonable to say that they will still be eating haphazardly two months from the date you bought this book. Don't be discouraged by that thought, because you're making progress. Remember that your nature expects immediate results, but planning demands time. Even though you're not on the system yet, the fact that your mind is centered on food and good meal combinations will automatically improve your dinners. When you've completed your menu-planning sheets, you deserve to celebrate!

Third Week (Remember to double the time again if you have a job outside your home or babies under two.)

The reason we could never follow the multitude of menu plans given in magazines was because much of the food suggested for a particular meal didn't fit our tastes, our pocketbooks, or our schedules. We'd get all excited about a picture on the cover, of a gorgeous table displaying tempting food. We'd snap up the issue with the intention of duplicating the feast for our friends and relatives. Unfortunately (and this happened over and over again), when we'd read the menu and the ingredients in each dish, we found them to be something like this:

Menu

Company Glazed Ham
Cranberried Salmon Ring
Dilled Baked Beans with Clam Sauce
Corn on the Cob
Mexican-Style Banana Bread

And, somehow, we never read past the glazed ham recipe to the dilled baked beans with clam sauce.

*COMPANY GLAZED HAM

12-14 lb.   smoked butt
for glaze, combine the juice from four
pomegranates (strain carefully)
2   tbsp. raisin wine (see recipe below)
1   tbsp. dark molasses
¼   cup clover honey
dash of cayenne pepper

Place butt fat side up on rack in shallow pan—do not cover or add water. Bake in slow oven (325°F) approximately 3–3¼ hours. Half an hour before time is up, remove butt from oven and pour fat drippings from pan. Score ham fat in diamond patterns—cut should be ¼″ deep. A strip of heavy paper, 12″ x 2″, is an easy guide for cutting parallel lines. After scoring, spoon glaze over meat until evenly coated. Now ham goes back in the oven for 30 minutes. For heavier coating, spoon glaze over butt several times.

Raisin Wine: Three months before you plan to make your glazed ham, pick 10 pounds of Concord grapes; extract juice as soon as possible. Put juice (approximately 2 qts.) in large crock, add 5 pounds sugar and ¼ cup brewer's yeast. Spread grape skins on several cookie sheets or stilted plywood drying frame. (See instructions in June 15 issue.) Place in a sunny spot. To ensure uniform drying, skins should be turned 3 times a day for 1 or 2 weeks, depending on the weather.

Make a cheesecloth bag. Use ⅛ yard cheesecloth stitched together on 3 sides, standard ⅝″ seams, leaving a ½″ casing at the top for a drawstring. (A white 100% cotton shoelace fitting a 5-hole athletic shoe works nicely.) Fill with the leaves of 2 coriander bushes,

---

*Please do not attempt to follow this recipe. We have not kitchen-tested, table-tested, family-tested, or guest-tested it. In fact, we haven't yet located any athletic shoes with shoelaces, a crock, or a thermometer—and that Fahrenheit-Celsius relationship just might be a bit off....

6 bay leaves, and 1 lb. of hops. Float in crock of juice mixture. The mixture will ferment in approximately 2 weeks if kept at a constant temperature of 85°F, 53°C.

Your menus have to be hand-picked by you and your family, and if somebody has a craving for raisin wine, let him fly to Napa Valley. You'll have a card file of family favorites, and in this third week, you'll be transferring those menus from the completed planning sheets onto 3x5 cards.

We use white cards for our menus. To do yours, write the menu in the center of the card with the main dish first. On the following page is an example of a menu card. In the upper left-hand corner, put the season that you'll be serving the menu (spring/summer or fall/winter). In the upper right-hand corner, put comments, such as quick, cheap, company, all-oven, barbecued, etc. In the center (top) write the category—beef, poultry, pork, lamb, seafood, specialty. Write the complete menu, taken from the Menu-Planning Sheets, in the center of the card.

On the back of this menu card, list ingredients needed at the store for the main dish ONLY. If the main dish was roast chicken, on the back of the menu card it might say: 1 large roasting chicken, garlic, olive oil, poultry seasoning—whatever you need to have on hand to make the roast chicken the way you like it. All the other ingredients for the side dish recipe, vegetable, salad, and dessert will either be in cookbooks, your recipe file, or, in the case of a dish you have in your head, on a 3x5 card with ingredients, filed in your card-file box in the ABCs section.

An example of an "in your head" dish is our mom's recipe for stuffed baked potatoes. We never, ever saw a recipe, because there never was one, so we memorized what Mom put into that dish. But since we were trying here to eliminate the need to think, we decided we should think just one more time and make a list of all the ingredients we would need if we were going to make Mom's stuffed potatoes. We then put that list on a 3x5 card and filed it in the ABCs—we file to the front and so does the Army—in front of either S for "stuffed" or, more likely, P for "potatoes."

Menu Card Example

S/S   POULTRY   Barbecued

Barbecued Chicken
Potato Salad
Broccoli
French Bread
Strawberries with
whipped cream

(white 3x5)

Reverse Side of Card

1 split fryer
barbecue sauce
oil
onion
vinegar
brown sugar
Dijon mustard
Worcestershire sauce
ketchup and chili powder

Tacos are another example. We all know what we have to get at the store to fix good tacos. But when you're at the store it's hard to remember all the items. Usually you'll come home minus the onions or the cheese.

All of these reference cards can be made up throughout the year as a particular meal is chosen. If you tried to make them all out in the third week, your brain would go out on you in the same way it does when you force it to remember things from the past, like what Beaver's father's name was on *Leave It to Beaver*, or who Superman—George Reeves— played in *Gone With the Wind*.*

Just make out the reference cards when the recipe is fresh in your mind.

As you complete a menu card check it off the menu-planning sheet.

At the end of the third week (sixth week, if you work outside your home) you'll have dozens of menu cards, depending on how many main dishes your family came up with, and you'll be ready to fill out the blank dividers and set up the rotating menu system.

Fourth Week

Start with your 3x5 file box, putting the supplies in this order:

1-31 dividers (to be discussed in Chapter Eight)
A blank divider labeled "Maintenance" (to be discussed
    in Chapter Eight)
12 blank dividers labeled as follows:

> S/S Beef
> S/S Pork
> S/S Poultry
> S/S Lamb
> S/S Fish
> S/S Specialty
> F/W Beef

*Ward Cleaver; one of the Tarleton twins.

F/W Pork
F/W Poultry
F/W Lamb
F/W Fish
F/W Specialty

A blank divider labeled "Freezer" (to be discussed in
   Chapter Seven)
A blank divider labeled "Crisis" (to be discussed in
   Chapter Ten)
ABC dividers, these will be used to alphabetize recipes
   by title, and "in head" ingredients for accompani-
   ments (reference cards)

Rainbow-colored cards can be put in the back of the box
for now. They'll be used as maintenance cards once you've
bailed out the kitchen and it's clean and organized.

File all of the white menu cards in front of their appropriate categories according to season.

Now you're ready to go shopping...but not for groceries.
It's time to buy a bulletin board. Every organized person
has one, and you'll need one on which to post your menu
cards. It should be big enough to display a calendar, messages,
and all seven 3x5s for the week. It should be sturdy but cute,
and permanently mounted in a centralized place in the
kitchen. If you buy the bulletin board and *fail to get it on
the wall*, all the menu cards may end up under the bed. If
the board's up, you'll put the cards on the board. With the
cards on the board you might as well say, "Welcome to
Sarah Tucker's Inn," and you know you'd better have the
whipped topping in the refrigerator. Creative people need
devices to keep them on the track, and the mounting of a
bulletin board is like a visual promise that you will follow
through with your commitment.

Fifth Week

You probably think that now we'll have you choose
seven menu cards, post them on the bulletin board, mark
your grocery list, and head to the store—NOT TRUE!

What would you do with all the stuff when you got it home? The kitchen's a mess; the cupboards are confused; the refrigerator is disgusting, and the freezer is frozen shut.

Keep eating as usual. . . . You're almost there, but you still have to get the kitchen ready to welcome the new food.

The fifth week will be spent bailing out, cleaning, organizing, and taking an inventory of the kitchen.

7
STARTING OVER

Saturday is a good day to start reaming out the kitchen. Friday night lay out some cute tight jeans, a Loni Anderson blouse, and some strappy high heels. You'll also need a colorful scarf that you'll tie Rhoda Morgenstern-style across your forehead. Once you're dressed Saturday morning, the idea is to get your husband to say, "Let's get a sitter tonight, and I'll take you out to dinner." The sooner he says it, the sooner you can change into Realityware (jogging suit, wrinkled bandanna, and tennis shoes). If you don't want to go the manipulatory route, throw something in the Crock-Pot™. Whichever way you choose, the point is, at the end of the day you are not going to feel like cooking, so take steps toward dinner before you start to clean.

Enter the kitchen with a scratch pad and a pen attached to yourself by a retractable coil. (You'll be jotting down all the things you'll need to make your kitchen more efficient.) We hope your dishes from the night before are done. You should start with a cleared table, clean counters, empty sink, empty dishwasher, and an empty garbage can.

Divide your kitchen into four areas: wet, hot, cold, and

dry. We'll explain later how every item in your kitchen will fall into one of these categories.

Each area will take at least a day to organize. You could take four days in a row and work nonstop, or devote one day a week to each area and have it perfect in a month. Either way you'll accomplish the same thing, so choose the easiest schedule for you and your family.

You won't be cleaning all of your cupboards at once; you'll be concentrating on one area at a time. That way you won't tear up more than you can put back, let alone clean.

If you remember any other time you've cleaned cupboards, the kitchen looked like a poorly organized rummage sale. The floor, counters, table, chairs, stove, and sink disappeared under the rubble.

We've decided that the sink—obviously in the wet area—is the best place to start cleaning. If you think about it, your kitchen sink is a testimony to your overall cleanliness. In fact, when a friend comes to the front door, you might as well take her straight to the sink, because sooner or later she'll have to throw away her gum, get a drink of water, or wash her hands. Next to the front door and the tile in front of the toilet, your kitchen sink is the most scrutinized area of your home. Visitors will judge that if your dishcloth is gray, so are your bra straps; if there's a ring in your sink, there's a ring in your bathtub; if your scouring pad is rusty and stuck to the bar of soap, then your paintbrushes are stiff and stuck in a coffee can somewhere; if that little basket thing in your sink has garbage in it, your lint trap is probably full of fuzz. Your company won't have to go beyond the wet area to guess what the rest of your life is like.

By now, if you are feeling disgusted with yourself, put a piece of gum in your mouth and go next door. After a little chitchat ask if you can get a drink of water and swiftly move to the kitchen.

Take note of the water spots on the faucets, stains in the porcelain, and wadded-up dishcloths in the sink. How about the counters? Are they covered with crumbs and clutter? In the midst of the bread crumbs are there tongue tracks in the peanut butter left on a table knife? Notice the thermos, frying pan, and cereal bowls in various stages of soaking. In the same way you determine age by counting the rings of a tree, count the rings in the sink to determine how long it's been since the last scouring.

Now ask to spit out your gum. When she puts her hand under your chin, you can go home knowing you're not alone. If, and this is a slight chance, her sink is immaculate, get out fast and go on to the next house. You will never find two clean sinks on the same block.

Feeling better, return to your own sink, guilt free and ready to start fresh.

There are some basic problems with all sink areas. Because sink manufacturers insist on that stupid indentation for holding a bar of soap, we homemakers have had to contend with soap slime for decades. Sink-makers have modified the indentation to allow water to drain off, but the soap always runs off with the water. Give up trying to get a bar of soap to stay put. On the scratch pad, write, "Soft-soap." Note the color container that would look best in your kitchen.

The first cupboard you'll organize is the one under the sink. You'll use our standard four-box method to help you decide what to do with each item as you come to it. One box is for throw-away—you could use your garbage can; one for put-away, one for give-away/sell, and one for storage.

Suppose you find a bag of rotten potatoes. Throw them away. Put the vaporizer and a can of paint in the put-away box (they go in the bathroom and the garage when you're finished cleaning). Put your collection of florist vases in the give-away/sell box. They can be exhibited at your next garage sale. Put the canning jars and the canner in the storage box, to be kept in a storage area outside of the kitchen. Don't stop until the whole cupboard is empty. Fill the sink with hot sudsy water to use as you clean. Spray disinfectant after scrubbing under the sink. If you want to line your shelves, use shelf paper or any leftover kitchen wallpaper you've saved, and attach it with double-sided tape. Scrubbing and disinfecting under the sink is a job that needs to be done once a week, preferably on garbage pickup day. You'll need a card to remind you of this job, but all maintenance cards will be made out later from the activity list (see Chapter Eight).

Cupboards filled with the appropriate items will be energy-efficient. However, we have a very important point to make before you start.

People born organized, like Ordell, are constantly studying time and motion. They love to chart their movement patterns. In their organizing books they caution us against wasting energy on needless steps. "When baking a pie," they warn, "five extra steps taken to reach a rolling pin put away in the wrong area may not seem so costly, but multiply those five steps by one pie a week and you've tallied up two hundred sixty steps. Two hundred sixty steps will take you around the block, and that's a long way to go to get a rolling pin."

What Ordell forgets is that every morning at 5:45 A.M., she jogs around the block twenty times, so what's the big deal? We don't deny that time and motion is a valid study, but we who are sidetracked need to take into consideration that we are extremists and so are the efficiency experts.

There is a middle of the road. Keep in mind that a little forethought when you are putting things into a clean cupboard will save you time later.

Now sit down in front of the bare cupboard and think "wet." (If at this point you have to go to the bathroom, do it now, but come right back.) We suggest that in the cupboard under the sink you keep cleaning supplies, a lined wastebasket, extra folded grocery sacks, rubber gloves, and a towel rack.

There are about six favorite cleaning products that we love, and we keep them under the sink in an empty soda pop bottle carton. Most cleaning containers will fit into a soda pop carrier; an eight-pack will allow room for six products, a rag, and a scrub brush. An old toothbrush is an excellent tool to keep in this cleaning caddy also. The smaller brush will work better to clean around drains, faucets, caulking, and grout. The idea for the cleaning caddy came from observing professional housekeepers in hotels. They don't run back and forth between the supply closet and the rooms to get linens, furniture polish, towels, and window cleaner. They use a cleaning cart that has everything they'll need.

You can use that same principle with the cardboard cleaning caddy. It can be carried from room to room, eliminating all unnecessary trips.

You can cover the pop carrier in contact paper if you want it to look pretty. The paper will also make it stronger. Pretty or not, it's a necessity for a sidetracked person.

When the cupboard under the sink is in order, move to the next section of the wet area. You will probably have one cupboard and one drawer in the area around the sink.

Below is a list of items we think belong in the wet area.

WET AREA INVENTORY

Cupboards:
cutting board
coffee maker
colander
Jell-O molds
water pitcher
watering can
cleaning supplies
waste basket
plastic garbage liners or grocery sacks

Drawers:
paring knife
sieve
peeler
garlic press
egg slicer
medication, pain relievers, vitamins, etc.
Band-Aids
big spoon
plant fertilizer
dishcloths

dish towels
hand lotion
rubber gloves

Attached to wall:
paper towel holder

Sink:
Softsoap

If you have small children, have a simple safety catch installed on the cupboard door (write it on the scratch pad as something to buy).

Let's pretend the next place you move to is the hot area (the stove, oven, and surrounding cupboards). This is where most of the tension in the home begins. The homemaker, after a tiring day, approaches the element with irritation, repulsion, and absolutely no idea of what to cook.

She'll often set the oven at 375° F, and in the back of her mind she'll be thinking, *eat in an hour.* If she uses the preheat feature, she'll be temporarily impressed with herself. She'll have the feeling of superiority that comes from planning ahead. Unfortunately, when she does think of something to fix, she'll forget to switch the selector to "bake." Scalloped potatoes become Crunch Top Char Tots when the basic scalloped potato recipe cooks full time on "preheat." If you use your preheat setting, be sure to add the word *char* to most of your recipe titles.

Often before she puts the selection in the oven, smoke from the remains of the previous meal can cause a catastrophe.

"Quick, grab the Odor Patrol."

"What?"

"The Odor Patrol, that little policeman on the windowsill. Take his boots off and wave him through the air."

"Whooh!"

"Now point him at the oven and push down on his hat."

"Oh, oh."

"Hurry, before the smoke alarm goes off."

She may even decide to turn off the oven and torch up

the barbecue. If she chooses to stay in and go through "burn off," she'll have to put up with at least fifteen minutes of fan time.

The sound of a kitchen fan has the same effect as somebody staring at you. You're still functional, but it's unnerving. Sometimes you don't realize how awful it is until it's been turned off. It's as nagging as a toddler jerking your hemline at a checkout stand or the tenor next to you singing off-key through the whole of "The Star-Spangled Banner."

To avoid excessive smoke inhalation in the future, you must now clean drip pans, ovens, and fan filters. In Chapter Eight we'll tell you how to keep them clean with a complete maintenance system.

When the hot area cupboards have been emptied and cleaned, don't put one thing back until you've examined it and asked yourself these three questions.

1. *Does it work?* If it's a pot, does the lid fit tightly and are the handles on securely? If it's an appliance, does the thermostat work? Are the attachments with it? Do you have the cord? If it's a potholder, is it worn through or too cutesy to be effective?

2. *Is it easy to clean?* A Crock-Pot™ without a removable crock will be used once and then be left to soak forever. Things that won't go through the dishwasher are a luxury you need to be careful of, like delicate hand washables you've worn once and never seen again. A brass, rosewood-handled au gratin pan will surely deprive your family of anything au gratin because of the special care it requires. Be honest with yourself: When was the last time you did a batch of hand washables? Keep that in mind when you buy new things for yourself or your kitchen.

3. *When was the last time you used it?* Have you used your automatic hot dog cooker lately? How about your doughnut-maker? When was the last time you fixed a hamburger with your single-hamburger maker or deep-fat fried one onion ring at a time in your mini fryer? One appliance—the stove—and a good pan can take the place of all these goofy Christmas presents you're storing.

Cupboards in the hot area should contain only those

items that have passed the examination and will be used near the stove or oven. Here is a list of the items we keep in these cupboards and drawers.

HOT AREA INVENTORY

Cupboards:
cutting board
small saucepan with lid
medium saucepan with lid
large kettle with lid
frying pan with lid
roasting rack
cooking spices (not too near the stove; heat causes
   flavor loss)
fire extinguisher
wok

Drawers:
butcher knife (meat)
serrated-edge knife (bread)
paring knife
wooden spoon
wire whip
spatula
mixing spoons
measuring spoons
measuring cups
meat thermometer
burn ointment
candy thermometer
pot holders

Drawers/Cupboards:
cooling racks

Cupboards/oven:
broiler pan

Because of the layout of your kitchen, you may not need duplicates of some items. An example would be if the dry and the hot area of your kitchen are adjacent, then it might be possible to keep measuring cups (an item you need in both areas) in a drawer or cupboard that can be reached while you are in either area.

Maintenance cards made in Chapter Eight will keep the hot area the way you want it.

Now you are ready to organize the cold area, the refrigerator and freezer.

The refrigerator is like a candy machine at a public swimming pool. It's a gathering place. The refrigerator is the first thing your kids hit when they come home from school. It's the first place your husband goes when he comes home from work. When you're thirsty in the middle of the night, it's like an oasis in a cowboy movie. Many a night we've felt like Poncho and Cisco, gratefully quenching our thirst from a full carton of milk. (If you're going to sneak milk out of the container in the middle of the night, keep it on a lower shelf and don't buy the gallon size. There's nothing worse than throwing a quarter of a cup of milk over your head in the dark and having to sneak back to bed in wet pajamas.)

In order to use your refrigerator effectively, you will need to keep it clean and organized.

Turn off the refrigerator and empty it. Dump anything that looks like it's capable of contaminating or attacking the rest of its neighbors.

As you go through this bail-out you will discover many rules you should have established but didn't. Make a list of rules as you clean. When you find something wrong think of a rule that would have avoided the mess in the first place.

For instance: three half-full glasses of milk on various shelves. No one ever finishes milk he didn't drink with a meal. He pours fresh.

Rule: Do not put half glasses of milk in the refrigerator. Pour less in the beginning.

Wash the racks in hot sudsy water with a little baking soda

added. Wash the inside of the refrigerator with the same cleaning solution. Replace the shelves.

Lower a rack containing milk, juice, and cold water, not just to prevent wet pajamas but so that children can reach the containers themselves.

We both have a lot to be grateful for. If we had been born sidetracked in the icebox age, we would have forgotten to empty the water pan. We would have neglected to have the ice cut off while we were on vacation, and then on our return we would have forgotten to call the guy to get it started up again. In short, we would basically have been confined to smoked, canned, or room temperature foods.

Now you can buy refrigerators with juice coming out of the door, ice plopping out on command, and extra energy-saving doors that nobody uses. Still, with all this innovation, even the most sophisticated refrigerators have vegetable crispers. Vegetable crispers operate on the same principle as the stupid soap indentation in sinks. They don't work.

Homemakers spend hours in the produce sections of their grocery stores, choosing the greenest lettuce, the firmest tomatoes, the reddest radishes, the ripest avocados, and the prettiest mushrooms, only to take them home and kill them in the crisper. Tomatoes get smooshed, mushrooms get bruised, bean sprouts turn brown, and what doesn't die in the crisper gets buried in the back behind the cottage cheese, leftover tuna casserole, dill pickles, mustard, and ketchup.

Most refrigerators have two crispers. We keep cans of pop in one and heads of lettuce and cabbage, corn on the cob, and other heavy produce in the other. The rest of the fresh vegetables—the delicate, expensive ones that are easily lost or squashed—hang in their plastic bags from shower curtain hooks. We put a tension rod—the kind that holds curtains inside a window casing—across the back of the refrigerator. Many plastic sacks of produce then hang like blouses on a clothes rack.

"Can I help you with anything?"

"Sure. Would you like to make the salad? The vegetables are hanging in the refrigerator."

People have questioned the convenience of our hanging produce, arguing that if it's in the back, it's hard to get to it. But something always has to be in the back, unless you have a walk-in refrigerator.

If you want to use this idea, measure the inside of your refrigerator and write the figure on your scratch pad, so you can get a rod that will fit. Also write down one package of plastic shower curtain hooks.

When you buy produce, we suggest that you trim and clean it before you hang it up. Your kids will be more inclined to snack on carrot and celery sticks if they are washed and cut in convenient-size pieces, and you will enjoy making salads when you don't have to take time to wash and drain the lettuce and vegetables.

When your refrigerator is clean and organized, start on the freezer. Although the freezer is probably not in your kitchen, we will discuss it now as part of the cold area. When we were little our parents had a big, white chest freezer in the utility room. When the motor turned on it shook the whole house and we used to lie on it and sing, thinking we sounded just like Eartha Kitt. We also pretended it was one of those machines at a reducing salon. Whenever we wanted to get anything out of the freezer, we had to force open the huge door and lean into it. We especially liked to chip the horrible-tasting ice that grew in it.

Mom had it stocked with fruits and vegetables from the garden, every meat a butcher could think of, and more. Since our dad loved to hunt and fish, we had venison, pheasant, goose, duck, salmon, trout, clams, and you name it. If Dad could catch it, it was in our freezer.

Mom let us make Kool-Aid and freeze it in ice cube trays, and when we grew up and got freezers of our own, that was about all we used them for.

As always, we had good intentions and visions of our uprights looking like the ones in the catalog or displayed in appliance stores, each shelf filled to capacity with every food imaginable. A Betty Furness fantasy land. Betty Furness could do a sixty-minute lecture on what we'd done to

our freezers. They were a mess! On first opening those
frozen tombs, the only thing visible was the freezer ice.
Where the kids had chipped away the icy white stuff there
was evidence of food, but it was like trying to identify the
lawn furniture after a heavy snowfall.

Braving the subzero temperatures, we attacked our freezer
wastelands and, like two dedicated anthropologists, slowly
uncovered our pasts. With numb and aching fingers, we
discovered mysterious bowls and containers of long-forgotten
leftovers. Everything was unlabeled, but after several hours
at room temperature, some things took on a vague resemblance of food we were familiar with. Everything was
spongy and dried up. We had to dump almost all of it. In
order to avoid this Siberian experience, you'll need to
defrost the freezer regularly (see the activity list on pp.
86–91).

When you get your freezer defrosted and completely
cleaned out, do something that goes totally against your
nature: Read the owner's manual. If you can't find it, and
you probably can't, ask for a replacement from the mer-
chant who carries your brand. If your freezer is old, your
manual may be outdated, and the ideas about "what to
freeze and how" may be too limited. If this is the case, we
suggest you go to the appliance department of a large store,
such as Sears or Wards, and ask if they have an extra
freezer owner's manual. Tell them, "My freezer is very old
and I'd like to study the ideas and innovations of the latest
Kenmore."

It's likely that you'll learn a lot and when the old freezer
forms its final frost, you'll be inclined to buy the appliance
you've already studied. Don't be concerned with operation
procedures. You've been operating in ignorance, just fine,
for years.

We established a rule that nothing could be put into our
clean, empty freezers without being labeled and entered on
pink 3x5 cards filed in front of the "Freezer" divider. If we
bought a five-pound roast, we would wrap it in white
freezer paper, date it, code it, and write the code on the
card. Let's say the first item you buy for your clean and

empty freezer is a five-pound rump roast. Rewrap it in white freezer paper and put a #1 on it in BLUE crayon. On a pink 3x5 card, put a #1 and write the date and the words "5 lb. rump roast." (See the example of a freezer card on p. 174.)

Remember the rule: Never put anything in the freezer without coding it and writing the code on the freezer cards. We said, "Use a blue crayon," because the cut of meat was beef. We use PURPLE crayon for poultry, RED for pork, BLACK for fish, and GREEN for anything else. Keep an eight-pack of crayons in a drawer along with freezer paper, freezer tape, foil, etc. It's easier to locate a package in the freezer when it's color-coded.

We keep roasts, whole chickens, turkeys, cornish game hens, and all large roasting packages on one shelf. We store chops and steaks, breads and rolls, desserts, and leftovers on separate shelves. We keep our frozen fruits, vegetables, and juices in the door shelves.

File all the freezer cards in your card file in front of the divider marked "Freezer." You will have a separate card for beef, pork, poultry, seafood, lamb, specialty breads, desserts, fruits, and vegetables. As you eat what you've frozen cross it off the card it was logged on. When the card gets filled up start another one.

The freezer compartment of the refrigerator will be used for food to be consumed right away. An inventory card isn't necessary because you can see everything that's in there.

With the cold area finished, move on to the final area to be organized, the dry area. It includes the pantry, china cupboard, and mixing center.

Remember to ask yourself the three questions: Does it work? Is it easy to clean? When was the last time you used it?

Be aware of the fact that you use your favorite things eighty percent of the time. The other items that you use only twenty percent of the time will probably be seasonal, like canning supplies, a Christmas tree cake pan, the turkey roaster, or cookie cutters.

The dry area includes the mixing, storage, and serving

sections. These three sections may or may not be next to each other. In fact, they probably are not. Since the dry area is the largest area in your kitchen, we are going to discuss each section separately.

The mixing section is the place where you will mix things. It's the place where you will make cakes, muffins, pancake batter, soufflés, salad dressings, etc. You could go crazy if you get too strict on the different areas and sections. Don't let questions get you confused, like, "I mix scrambled eggs, so should I do it only in the mixing area?" or "I have to add two tablespoons of water to this pastry, so should I be in the wet area?" You can't fix scrambled eggs in the mixing section unless you like them raw, and if you mixed all recipes that called for water in the wet area, then you'd have to mix recipes that called for milk in the cold area. The idea of dividing your kitchen into the different areas is only to give you a basic guideline.

The mixing section should have the following inventory.

MIXING SECTION INVENTORY

Cupboards:
    set of mixing bowls
    measuring cups (liquid and dry)
    mixer (keep beaters and bowls with mixer)
    muffin pans
    9" x 13" cake pan
    2 round 8" cake pans
    2 10" pie dishes
    2 loaf pans
    cookie sheets

Baking Staples:
    spices
    shortening
    baking soda
    baking powder
    salt

brown sugar
vanilla
(Sugar and flour should be in attractive canisters on the
counter in the mixing area.)

Drawers:

mixing spoons
rubber spatula
measuring spoons
wire whip
rolling pin
grater
spreading knife (for frosting)

The storage section includes the pantry (cupboards for
food), all the high cupboards, and the corners in kitchens
where two cupboards meet.

If your pantry has deep shelves, you will need to invest
in some lazy Susans. There are pull-out shelves you can
buy ready-made that attach to your existing shelves. The
important thing is to be able to get to the food you put in
the back. There is nothing more irritating than to have to
stick your head in a dark cupboard and try to find a can of
cream of chicken soup.

If you are under five feet four inches tall, use the high
shelves for bulk storage. It's a good idea to keep a little
child's stepstool nearby for your younger children when
they help and for you when you need to reach the top
shelves.

We call the third area the Bermuda Triangle. In corners
where two cupboards meet, one cupboard always has space
that is hard to get to. Use that place for storage. For
example, the corner cupboard in the dry area might have a
shelf for baking supplies. A collection of cookie cutters or
the birthday cake platter, both used infrequently, could be
put back in the Bermuda Triangle. Whenever you box
things into a hard-to-reach space, do it with large utensils.
It's easier to remove an angel food cake pan and a bundt

pan to reach the Triangle than it is to move a set of measuring cups or mixing bowls, shortening, baking soda, salt, or vanilla.

STORAGE SECTION INVENTORY

Cupboards/Pantry:
    canned foods
    bottled goods
    staples (see grocery list in appendix)

High Cupboards &
Bermuda Triangle:
    surplus food in bulk quantities
    seasonal items (turkey roaster, witch cake pan, the
    canner, Christmas cookie cutters)

There is one other thing that will go into storage—the "Gift Box." It will contain all of the presents that you'll never use but can't throw away because it would hurt someone's feelings.

Put the indecent-looking nutcracker from the South Seas into the box, along with the giant resin starfish ashtray with sparkles embedded in it and the kitchen clock that wags its tail and blinks its eyes.

Store them in the box outside of the kitchen, far enough away so that they can't be seen but close enough to get to if a benefactor's car pulls into the driveway.

We have divided the dry area drawers into eight categories. If you don't have eight separate drawers, you will of course combine things, but consider our divisions when you organize your own dry area.

The eight drawers are silverware, utensil, kid, paper, deli, telephone, bread, and junk, and contain the items listed below.

Silverware Drawer:
    flatware

serving spoons
steak knives

Utensil Drawer:

The utensil drawer is explained in the Mixing Section
Inventory. It should contain:
mixing spoons
rubber spatula
measuring spoons
wire whip
rolling pin
grater
spreading knife (for frosting)

Kid Drawer:

ice-cream scoop
straws
coupons and contest offers
toothpicks
napkins
Band-Aids
bottle openers
lunch bags
plastic wrap

Paper Drawer:

plastic wrap
aluminum foil
Baggies
Ziploc bags
masking tape
freezer paper
freezer bags
8-pack of crayons

Deli Drawer:

can opener
bottle opener

bottle stoppers
bar tools—jiggers, stir sticks, etc.
corkscrew
cheese slicer
sharp knife
toothpicks
cocktail napkins

Telephone Drawer:
phone book
pencils/pens
3x5 scratch pad
calendar
paper clips
baby-sitter information
needles, thread, glue (If you keep these items by the phone, you can mend while you talk.)
letter opener
stapler
rubber bands

Bread Drawer:
bread
English muffins
basket
napkins

Junk Drawer:
2 screwdrivers (regular and Phillips)
pliers
hammer
picture nails
duct tape
electricians tape (plastic)
crescent wrench
faucet repair kit
first aid kit
flashlight

    rubber bands
    Band-Aids

If you like the idea of having a kid drawer, you might consider having a kid cupboard.

Kid Cupboard:
    cold cereal
    popcorn and popcorn popper
    ice-cream cones
    toaster
    paper cups

The picnic basket is part of storage because it isn't usually used all year. If you have a cute one, you might want to leave it out.

Picnic Basket: (Use a produce box if you don't have a real wicker basket. If you are a romantic, as we are, put it on your scratch pad to buy.)
    red-and-white checkered tablecloth
    corkscrew
    paper plates
    plastic silverware
    napkins
    can opener
    bottle opener

The serving section includes the china cupboard, silverware drawer (see p. 72), and table area. Keep tablecloths, place mats, candles, and centerpieces in the dining room. If you don't have a dining room, you will need another drawer in your kitchen.

As you clean and organize all the areas in your kitchen, you will come across duplicates: knives, spoons, corkscrews, bottle openers, etc. Before you put them in the give-away/sell box think about using them in other areas. For example, an extra can opener could go in the picnic basket.

When you've finished with all four areas you should have quite a list of things you need to buy, written on your scratch pad. Don't limit your list to the things you can afford today. The first step toward a new purchase is a plan. If you want new dining room furniture, write it down. If you need a set of matching dishes, write it down. If you want a dishwasher, a freezer, or a complete kitchen demolition and remodeling, write it down.

When your kitchen is perfect you'll have the feeling of pride that comes with accomplishment. You'll toy with the idea of calling your second grade teacher to come and see what you've done, but she lives at Tranquil Terrace, a rest home, and you'd hate to disturb her, so you assemble your family instead.

With the grace of a starlet demonstrating a kitchen prize on *Let's Make a Deal* or *The Price Is Right*, you move through each area, pulling out drawers, opening cupboards, and holding up shiny appliances you've found the cords to. As you make a brazen display of the new kitchen to the rest of the family, behind the pretension or order lurks the truth about how it'll look in a month.

Sidetrackers don't like to put things back where they belong. It isn't necessarily a rebellious attitude, although we did hear that phrase millions of times from our mothers. Part of our failure to put things back where they belong is that we are so creative. We can find so many other places where the same things will fit. The ironing board, for instance, can slide neatly under the bed, in between the refrigerator and the wall, or behind the living room drapes. We have also discovered that we don't have to confine an activity to one room. We can get dressed in the kitchen, eat in the bedroom, and put on our makeup in the car. In our slob days the only thing that went back to where it belonged in the kitchen was the receiver on the telephone, and that was only because it was attached to a cord.

Our flexibility and creativity make life interesting but chaotic. Remember, the only reason to get organized is to have more free time and peace of mind.

The momentary elation of accidentally stumbling onto

the missing pair of scissors while groping for a map in the glove compartment—you wrapped a gift at stoplights on the way to a wedding shower—cannot offset the irritation of racing from the sewing basket to the junk drawer to the desk and finally having to improvise. How many times have you sawed off the end of the puppy's flea collar with a nail file? Chiseled through one of those tough plastic price tag deals with your teeth? Cut out a pantsuit with your kindergartner's blunt-ends, or tried to tear coupons with precision?

Have you ever tried to pick a bouquet of roses without a pair of scissors? Whenever we've gone out to gather roses from the garden, we've had a romantic vision of ourselves with a basket on our arm, wearing a wide-brimmed sun bonnet and a long flowing white dress, like in those slow-motion deodorant commercials. Roses don't snap. They must be carefully snipped with very sharp scissors, at a slant, in just the right place (see p. 67 of *The Serious Rose Growers Guide*). Any other way is criminal. We've raped our bushes trying to get the blooms without scissors. Breaking off the stems requires the same back-and-forth motion you use to break apart a coat hanger when you need a piece of wire to get into the car because you can't find your keys.

Not putting things back where they belong wastes time. Part of the reason things don't go back where they belong is that there is no established place. Now that you have established a place for everything in the kitchen, you need to get it in writing.

The next thing we are going to tell you to do will make you wild. You are going to read it and go unconscious, because your mind will blank out and you'll think about the weekend you spent at the beach or the dress you tried on that made you look ten pounds lighter. At the end of the statement you will regain consciousness and realize that you didn't understand the last group of words; that somehow your mind wandered a bit . . . so you'll reread it, and as your eyes read every word without skipping a single one, your mind will take off again. This time to what might have been if you'd married someone else, and how jealous you are of Kathy, because she gets to go on a cruise. When you reread it the third time you still won't get it; in fact, the third reading will be out loud and very slow, which will cause your mind to induce drastic measures. You will become thirsty and a little bit nauseated because of unexpected hunger pains. You'll have to go to the bathroom. You'll put the book down. Several hours later you'll spend fifteen minutes looking for the book because you didn't put it back where it belongs. Feeling that you've hit a technical snag, a psychological block—a left brain blowout—you'll attempt to read it one more time. Knowing you'll have to read this four times before it'll sink in, we've written it for you four times:

On a pink 3x5 card write down the contents of each clean and organized cupboard or drawer and tape the card to the inside.

On a pink 3x5 card write down the contents of each clean and organized cupboard or drawer and tape the card to the inside.

On a pink 3x5 card write down the contents of each clean and organized cupboard or drawer and tape the card to the inside.

On a pink 3x5 card write down the contents of each clean and organized cupboard or drawer and tape the card to the inside.

From now on you will put things back where they belong.

8

MAINTENANCE

We tried to think of a funny title for this chapter, but there is not one drop of humor in maintenance.

Once the entire kitchen is thoroughly clean and organized, you'll want to keep it that way. You will use the activity list at the end of this chapter (pp. 86–91) to make out maintenance cards that will help you keep your kitchen in order. The list is divided into the four areas—wet, hot, cold, and dry—plus it contains any other miscellaneous jobs that need to be done regularly. We have given you the frequency of each job according to a middle-of-the-road standard of cleanliness. Each job has also been timed. If the job takes less than ten minutes, it should be considered a mini-job and can be done while dinner cooks, while you talk on the phone, or any time you have a free moment and find yourself in the kitchen. Note: A long stretch cord for your kitchen telephone will enable you to gossip and work at the same time.

If you have children, many of the jobs can be part of their home responsibilities. On the activity list, we have given an average age at which a child can do each job successfully. The last column on the list will tell you which color each 3x5 maintenance card should be. Jobs that will be done daily will be YELLOW; weekly jobs will be BLUE, and monthly, seasonal, or yearly jobs will be WHITE. (All inventory cards are PINK.) Make any personal adjustments on the activity list before you start filling out the cards.

Using the appropriate-colored 3x5, you will make out one maintenance card for each job. (See our example of a maintenance card on p. 85.)

To schedule maintenance you'll need to make out a Maintenance Plan that will be based on a rotating five-week schedule. (See our example on p. 86.)

Each week, let's say on Saturday, when the family is available to help, you will focus on one area. For purposes of explanation we'll make week one the wet area, week two the hot area, week three the cold area, week four the dry area, and the fifth week for miscellaneous. An easy way to keep the sequence in mind is to start at the kitchen sink and work clockwise.

We've also broken the week down by area. Monday is wet, Tuesday hot, Wednesday cold, Thursday dry, Friday miscellaneous, and Saturday is designated as a family work day. You can adjust the plan any way you think will suit your personal circumstances. The sequence we have given you corresponds to the layout of our kitchens. To make your plan, start at the kitchen sink by assigning the wet area to week one. The next clockwise area will be assigned to the second week, and so on. When you've made your own plan put it on a white 3x5 card and paste it to the lid of your card file. You'll also need a small yearly calendar that you'll put in the front of the box.

In Chapter Six we had you set up your card file with 1-31 dividers in the front. Take them out now and arrange them so that the current date is in front. At the end of each day rotate that divider to the back, and the next day's date will come forward. Always keep the current date in the front of the card file.

Now make three piles of cards according to their color. Set the stack of white ones aside to file last. Begin with the yellow (daily) maintenance cards. File them in front of today's date if the job has not been done yet today. Daily jobs already completed can be filed in front of tomorrow's date. File yellow every-other-day cards in front of today's date if they haven't been done, or the day after tomorrow if they're already completed.

Now sort the blue cards, taking out any mini-job cards from the pile. Since these jobs all take ten minutes or less, they can be done during the week according to their area. Refer to your Maintenance Plan and file on the appropriate days. Don't file any blue cards beyond seven days unless they are to be done every other week, in which case you have fourteen days from the current date. Blue cards that require more than ten minutes are the "heavies" and will need to be scheduled on the family work day—(Saturday) —for distribution.

Finally you're ready to file the white cards. A job such as cleaning the cutting board would be scheduled for week one when the focus is the wet area. Since it is a mini-job— (ten minutes or less)—it will be filed during the first week on the wet area day—(Monday). File the card in front of Monday's date in your first week.

The monthly jobs of scouring drip pans and rims and cleaning the clock on the stove will be done during week two when the focus is on the hot area; cleaning the stove takes about forty-five minutes, so it is not a mini-job. It will have to be scheduled for the family work day. Putting the fan's filter through the dishwasher, however, will only take a minute. It can be done on Tuesday, the hot area day of the second week.

Because cleaning the top of the refrigerator is a monthly job and because the refrigerator is in the cold area, that job will be scheduled during the third week. As a mini-job, it will fall on Wednesday—cold area day.

The fourth week will be devoted to monthly jobs in the dry area, like straightening drawers and cupboards and cleaning small appliances. Remember to schedule all mini-jobs during the week according to the area they're in, and to schedule the more time-consuming jobs on the family work day.

Week five will be the miscellaneous week for monthly jobs like cleaning canisters, knickknacks, or the telephone. Schedule all miscellaneous jobs that take more than ten minutes for the family work day; the miscellaneous mini-jobs will fall on Friday.

Any maintenance card that needs to be done every other month, seasonally or yearly, regardless of its focus area, will be filed in front of the divider marked "Maintenance." This divider goes behind the 1-31 dividers in the file box. You will check the Maintenance divider at the end of each month, choosing one or two cards. Make out a tickler card that says "Check Maintenance," and file it in front of the thirty-first. Always keep it there as a reminder.

When you have chosen a job from the Maintenance divider, schedule it according to its focus area. Defrosting the freezer, for instance, should be scheduled for the week when the focus is on the cold area—week three. Since it is a big job, it will be filed on the family work day. Once the job is finished the card is dated and goes back to the Mainte-nance divider behind the other cards.

We suggest that if you're on our total housekeeping system from our first book, you keep your kitchen mainte-nance cards separate from your other household cards. This will mean having a kitchen card file with menus, recipes, freezer inventory, and kitchen maintenance cards, plus your original card file for the rest of the house. On the family work day you take charge of the kitchen while delegating other jobs in the house to other family members.

Sometimes housework can be overwhelming, but we've always been able to put it into the proper perspective. It's easy to remember our slob days when nothing was ever done. When we compare them to now, we realize how much better everything is.

So if one week we have to skip something, we do it

without guilt. The job is rescheduled, not neglected. We file it and forget it as if it had been done. Organized people say that work is love made visible and it's true, but so is taking time out to play with your children, sitting down with your husband to watch *Hill Street Blues*, taking your mom out to lunch, or writing a funny letter to a friend. All of these things show love. Ten years from now who will care whether or not you cleaned your knickknacks on Friday of the fifth week of every month? When your kids are grown will they remember bitterly how you abandoned the wet area one weekend to go to the beach? Will your husband look back on your life together and praise you for your religious devotion to your card file?

Time is the only thing in life that's given out equally to everyone. Being organized and having a maintenance schedule will save so much time. No more wasted moments looking for things. No more mental energy lost because your work is howling at you when you try to rest. No more leaving spills to harden until you have to chisel at them for hours. No more leaving dishes after dinner to crust over and then spending an extra twenty minutes in the morning, scrubbing. No more doing an autopsy on leftovers stashed in the refrigerator. No more loping through the supermarket at 5 P.M., trying frantically to spot something good for dinner.

We used to do all those things. We used to make work for ourselves, but our disorganization didn't mean we were any less loving. Our granny had a simple yet profound way of looking at life. She'd hear a problem and then have one of three things to say about it. It didn't matter what the problem was; one of her three responses would take care of it. Having had only an eighth-grade education, she used bad English, but her words were wise. She'd say:

1. "It don't matter."
2. "He don't mean nothin' by that."
3. We can't tell you the third one. She reserved this one for people like Hitler.

You could go to her and say, "My husband just ran off to Tahiti with his secretary," and she'd say, "Oh, honey, he don't mean nothin' by that." You could tell her you lost your wallet and all the grocery money was in it, and she'd say, "It don't matter." The next time you have to skip a card remember Granny, because you don't mean nothin' by it and, besides, it just don't matter.

Maintenance Plan

```
Weekly                              25 Min.



                WASH KITCHEN FLOOR



Vacuum first                        Delegate
Use Spic and Span                   14 Yrs.


```

Blue Card

Maintenance Plan

Week One—Wet Area	Mon.—Wet
Week Two—Hot Area	Tues.—Hot
Week Three—Cold Area	Wed.—Cold
Week Four—Dry Area	Thurs.—Dry
Week Five—Miscellaneous	Fri.—Miscellaneous

Sat.—Family Work Day

WET

Job	Frequency	Time Est.	Mini	Children	Color
Change dishcloth	(D)	2 Min.	X	4 Yr.	(Y)
Wash window over sink	(W)	7 Min.	X	9 Yr.	(B)
Fill dishwasher/wash pots and pans	(D)	20 Min.		8 Yr.	(Y)
Empty dishwasher	(D)	5 Min.	X	6 Yr.	(Y)
Clean/polish dishwasher door	(W)	3 Min.	X	6 Yr.	(B)
Scour sink/polish fixtures	(D)	3 Min.	X	7 Yr.	(Y)
Empty garbage/clean under sink	(D)	5 Min.	X	6 Yr.	(Y)
Garbage pickup day	(W)	5 Min.	X	8 Yr.	(B)
Clean cutting board	(M)	10 Min.	X	8 Yr.	(W)
Empty and wash wet area cupboards	(S)	30 Min.		10 Yr.	(W)
Empty and wash wet area drawers	(S)	30 Min.		10 Yr.	(W)
Replace wet area inventory cards	(2/Y)	1 Hr.			(P)

HOT

Job	Fre-quency	Time Est.	Mini	Chil-dren	Color
Clean stove top	(M)	45 Min.		14 Yr.	(W)
Clean range hood and fan	(M)	30 Min.		14 Yr.	(W)
Wash fan filter	(M)	2 Min.	X	8 Yr.	(W)
Clean self-cleaning oven inside/outside	(W)	5 Min.	X		(B)
Clean regular oven inside/outside	(M)	30 Min.			(W)
Clean microwave inside/outside	(W)	5 Min.	X	10 Yr.	(B)
Empty and wash hot area drawers	(S)	30 Min.		10 Yr.	(W)
Empty and wash hot area cupboards	(S)	30 Min.		10 Yr.	(W)
Replace hot area inventory cards	(2/Y)	1 Hr.			(P)

COLD

Job	Fre-quency	Time Est.	Mini	Chil-dren	Color
Defrost freezer	(2/Y)	1 Hr.			(W)
Clean freezer outside/top	(M)	5 Min.	X	8 Yr.	(W)
Defrost freezer com-partment of refrigerator	(2/Y)	30 Min.			(W)
Clean refrigerator outside/top	(M)	5 Min.	X	8 Yr.	(W)
Clean refrigerator inside	(W)	15 Min.		12 Yr.	(B)
Clean refrigerator drip pan	(S)	5 Min.	X	12 Yr.	(W)
Empty and wash cold area drawers	(S)	30 Min.		10 Yr.	(W)
Empty and wash cold area cup-boards	(S)	30 Min.		10 Yr.	(W)
Replace cold area inventory cards	(2/Y)	1 Hr.			(P)

DRY

Job	Fre-quency	Time Est.	Mini	Chil-dren	Color
Clean small appliances	(M)	10 Min.	X	10 Yr.	(W)
Empty and wash dry area drawers	(S)	30 Min.		10 Yr.	(W)
Empty and wash pantry cupboards	(S)	30 Min.		10 Yr.	(W)
Empty and wash all dry area cupboards	(S)	30 Min.		10 Yr.	(W)
Replace inventory cards	(2/Y)	1 Hr.			(P)

MISCELLANEOUS

Job	Fre-quency	Time Est.	Mini	Chil-dren	Color
Baking	(W)	2 Hr.		10 Yr.	(B)
Prepare meals	(D)	30 Min.		14 Yr.	(Y)
Set table	(D)	5 Min.	X	5 Yr.	(Y)
Choose menus for week	(W)	10 Min.	X	14 Yr.	(B)
Mark grocery list	(W)	5 Min.	X	14 Yr.	(B)
Grocery shopping	(W)	1 Hr.		14 Yr.	(B)
Wash knickknacks/ canisters	(M)	10 Min.	X	12 Yr.	(W)
Wash walls/paint	(Y)				(W)
Wash ceiling/paint	(Y)				(W)
Polish woodwork	(S)	2 Hr.		12 Yr.	(W)
Wash/dry clean curtains	(S)				(W)
Get cobwebs	(S)	5 Min.	X	12 Yr.	(W)
Clean light fixtures	(S)	10 Min.	X		(W)
Clean fingerprints on light switches	(W)	5 Min.	X	6 Yr.	(B)
Clean telephone	(M)	10 Min.	X	8 Yr.	(W)
Wash kitchen table and chairs	(D)	5 Min.	X	6 Yr.	(Y)
Wash/polish countertops	(D)	5 Min.	X	8 Yr.	(Y)
Polish silver and copper	(S)			10 Yr.	(W)

MISCELLANEOUS (cont'd.)

Job	Fre-quency	Time Est.	Mini	Chil-dren	Color
Sweep/damp mop floor	(D)	10 Min.	X	8 Yr.	(Y)
Wash floor	(W)	25 Min.		14 Yr.	(B)
Strip old wax	(S)	45 Min.		14 Yr.	(W)
Shake scatter rugs	(D)	10 Min.	X	4 Yr.	(Y)
Vacuum kitchen carpet	(D)	10 Min.	X	4 Yr.	(Y)
Shampoo kitchen carpet	(2/Y)	1 Hr.			(W)

*ESTABLISH THESE HABITS

——— Cook in an apron.

——— Fill the dishwasher and turn it on before bed.

——— As you empty the dishwasher set the table for the next meal.

——— Post 7 menu cards on grocery day.

——— Wipe up spills as they occur.

——— Delegate kitchen cards to each child daily.

——— Work with the children while preparing meals.

——— Listen to the children at the dinner table.

——— Try a new recipe each month.

——— Put at least 3 crisis meals in the freezer each week.

——— Ask for and accept help.

——— Consider the cleanup as part of the meal.

——— Serve balanced meals (2 milk servings, 2 meats, 4 fruits and vegetables, 4 grains).

——— Serve dinner on time.

——— Look pretty for dinner.

——— Clean off counters and soak pots and pans before sitting down to dinner.

——— Fill the sink with hot sudsy water before starting to prepare the meal.

——— Invite someone to share a meal once a month.

——— Have the refrigerator clean before getting groceries.

——— Wrap foods and code properly before putting them in the freezer.

——— Replace the dishcloth with a clean one daily.

——— Scour and polish the sink daily.

——— Empty the garbage and replace the liner daily.

——— Put things back neatly where they belong.

———————————

*Organized people have developed an army of good work habits. According to Dr. Maxwell Maltz in his book *Psycho-Cybernetics*, it takes only twenty-one days to establish a new habit.

THIS LITTLE PIGGY WENT TO MARKET

When your kitchen is just the way you want it, you're ready to choose seven menu cards, make a grocery list, and head to the market.

When you choose your menus, first check your calendar for upcoming events that would affect the week. For example, if the kids are going on a weekend camping trip with their grandparents, it'd be smart to pick out a "Romantic" menu card (see example below) for one of your meals.

S/S	BEEF	Romantic
	Steak Diane	
	Baked Potatoes	
	Caesar Salad	
	Homemade Rolls	
	Chocolate Mousse	

When deciding on your seven menus look over the advertised specials in the newspaper. Pick main dishes for the week according to what's on sale. Mark your grocery list as you go.

If a special occasion is coming up, you can see it on the calendar and plan accordingly. Before the big whoop-de-do gear down into nothing but "Cheap" cards (see example below), so you'll have extra money to spend on the party.

S/S	PORK	Cheap

Hot Dogs and Buns
Potato Chips
Baked Beans
Carrot and Celery Sticks
Popsicles

The family won't complain, because they'll know there will be a company dinner soon.

When you're using the menu card system you can easily jockey the cards to fit your budget and circumstances. When you're going to feed an additional thirty people at a special get-together, you need to conserve for the rest of the week. This doesn't mean the family will have to starve; they'll just have to eat meals that don't cost very much.

Planning the party menu will be easy. You can choose from several cards that would be nice for company (see example on following page).

Keep it simple, and when someone says, "What can I bring?" give him or her a choice from the menu card. If you want to keep all the credit for the meal to yourself, tell your guests they can't bring anything, but you must be prepared to spend a lot more time in the kitchen.

S/S   **BEEF**   Company

Shish Kebabs
Rice Pilaf
Salad Bar
Summer Fruit Platter
Sour Dough Rolls
Apple Pie and Ice Cream

Remember, we picked the menu card after we consulted the ads. Since beef was on sale, it would have been foolish to choose a menu card with chicken for the main dish.

You can use some of the money you've saved toward some conveniences that will make a big difference in time and work. For instance, instead of taking hours to slice cold cuts and finger foods like radish roses or carrot and celery sticks for an hors d'oeuvre tray, call the neighborhood deli and have the platter made up for you. Your husband can swing by and get it on his way home from work. Fruit platters are also available at a reasonable cost. If you tried to duplicate the wide variety of fresh summer fruits and cheeses that your deli can provide, the cost would be prohibitive, not to mention the time you'd waste peeling and pitting. The time saved is worth the money, and the money is available because you've bought things on sale and planned.

Choose a simple menu card for the day after the feast (see example below). You can substitute leftovers from the party for any similar food group listed on the chosen card.

S/S   **BEEF**   Leftover

Beef and Rice Casserole
Green Salad
Corn
Hot Rolls
Mixed Fruit with Cream

With your grocery list marked, you're finally ready to go marketing.

There are professional careers in marketing. People go to college and graduate with doctorates in the field. But for the majority of us, our education in marketing consists of following our mothers around the grocery store.

In high school we learned more about the stock market than we did about the supermarket. We even studied charts and graphs and tried to understand the gross national product (who picks the grossest item and gives it national acclaim?).

With all the attention on the stock market, you'd think the country revolves on ticker tape. We homemakers know it revolves on the tape that comes out of grocery store cash registers.

There should be a college course on how to go to the store and come out with only what you need.

We are as vulnerable at a grocery store as we are with our kids on the midway at a fair. American merchants are more subtle than concessionaires, but don't be fooled by their soft sell. The grocery industry spends millions of dollars on advertising to tell you what you should buy before you even leave your home. Then when you get to the store, you pass a display of toilet paper, and for some reason you just have to squeeze it as you put it in your cart. (Ten years ago that would never have entered your mind.) You come to a shelf of cake mixes and a melody pops into your head, courtesy of Pillsbury. There's an enormous poster of Mrs. Olson hanging from the ceiling, and you find yourself in the coffee aisle, needing caffeine when you've been de-caffeinated. Mechanical pineapples do the hula and lure you into the produce section while Madge dunks a home-maker's hand into a bowl of liquid detergent over and over and over again. You don't realize she's mesmerized you until the checker rings up the several bottles of green liquid you put into your cart.

If you get out of the store without succumbing to all of the posthypnotic suggestions, then you probably don't have a TV or radio. Most likely you'll fill up your basket like a little robot that has been programmed in advance to buy certain advertised products.

Another obstacle influencing the shopper is the demo lady. She'll hand you samples of sausage pizza and the leading soft drink. Then with food and drink in both hands, you'll have to push your grocery cart down the aisle with your stomach. Clever grocers know that the smell of food cooking will make you hungry, if you aren't already, and hunger will make you fill up your cart with more food.

Millions of dollars are also spent putting products at the homemaker's eye level. Manufacturers instruct their salesmen on ways to monopolize the eye-level area. Every food salesman learns in training that the average female shopper is five feet four and a half inches tall. By subtracting three inches for the forehead, the salesmen arrive at the precise height at which to place their line of products.

Prime shelf space is fought over. To get it, salesmen will bribe grocers with trips to Long Beach, or car blankets and barbecues. They also change the shelves when their competitors aren't looking.

The next time you go to the grocery store walk down the aisles one by one and look at what you see at eye level. If you are five feet four and a half inches tall and your eyes are in the right place, you will see the result of all that money, time, energy, worry, bribery, pleading, rearranging, and fighting. You can picture your friendly grocer cozy under a red plaid blanket, in front of his barbecue at the beach. And it's all for you.

The only things that won't be found at the homemaker's eye level are candies, toys, cookies, crayons, and funny books. That's because they are at the children's eye level. Notice that razors, shaving lotion, flashlights, and lunch boxes are up high for Macho Shopper.

If the shopper makes it through her friendly neighborhood grocery store without losing control, she has one final hurdle: the checkout counter. Here is the grocer's last chance to make another sale. There are tabloids with tempting titles like "Famous Star Tells What She Did to the President" or "Old Dog Digs Up Dead Master's Fortune."

Necessities such as Excedrin and Cope—often needed after the grocery store experience—vitamins, breath mints, and deodorant are pushed at her. Beef jerky is right in the way of the place to write a check. Now her children begin to bag. The gum, balloons, and candy are too much!

There are three kinds of checkout counters, but they all have the same enticements. There's the conveyor belt type, where the shopper feverishly unloads her own cart while the speedy checker runs a tab that cannot be verified. It's impossible to check charges while hanging over a grocery cart.

There's also the traditional checkout counter, with a checker who unloads your cart for you while he/she calls out prices on each item. Here you'll be pleased to find a real box boy who'll actually carry your groceries and help you find your car.

The third type of checkout counter is the Jiffy Line, where you can only have eight items or fewer, and you must have cash. At the Jiffy Line you'll usually come upon a checker trainee who's trying to get the knack of cash register operation. A sidetracked person will rarely take advantage of the Jiffy Line because she never has cash. She may not even have the checkbook, in which case the store manager will have to be called to put her groceries in the cooler while she rushes home to get it.

On the way out of the store, if the posters, jingles, demos, and motors have worn her down, the shopper will probably consent to letting her kids go on the rocket ride or throw a quarter away on a trinket machine for a chance at a fluorescent spy ring or rubber snake.

Finally, after about two hours, the ordeal is over. The homemaker, dazed and weak, heads for home, while her children gnaw on their pepperoni sticks amid a dozen bags of crushed groceries stuffed in the backseat. (The trunk was full of soda pop bottles they forgot to return.)

When we were disorganized, returning bottles was an annual fiasco. Although the return was quite profitable, usually into six figures, it was a hassle we vowed to resolve. Loading them into the car was a family project that took several hours and was rewarded with a celebration feast. Just because the soda pop bottles were loaded into the car didn't necessarily mean they were taken back to the store the same day. When the big day finally did come the bottles were all over the trunk, because of sharp turns and sudden stops. The station wagon had a coating of sticky film that was a combination of Pepsi, Dr Pepper, and 7-Up. We were familiar with several species of cola-loving insects.

We've felt so guilty about the condition in which we returned our bottles. In a year, spiders can build entire condominiums in a six-pack. They can display an engineering creativity that goes beyond human imagination when given the time and materials. Our kids played with the bottles we stored in the garage. They filled them with mud, sand, grass, seeds, and anything they could find that was small enough to be pushed inside.

Ring...ring...

"Hello."

"Oh, Sissy, you should see Ordell's bottles."

"What bottles?"

"Her empty soda pop bottles. She only has six of them. She told me she rinses a bottle out the instant she pours the pop over ice."

"She does?"

"Yeah, she takes pride in her sparkling returns."

"Did she see in your garage?"

"No, thank goodness. She couldn't handle it."

"Imagine how the soda pop people appreciate her."

"Do you think they have to throw our bottles out sometimes?"

"Probably. I've been tempted to take mine to a store across town where I wouldn't be recognized."

Now that we're organized, even our soda pop bottles are under control.

It's obvious that grocery shopping can be depressing and exhausting and your kids can either be an asset or a liability. You can avoid ninety percent of the hassle by shopping with an organized list and getting your children to help you.

Be very selective about the store you choose to patronize. Some stores have a depressing atmosphere in which tempers are short, shelves are messy, produce is wilted, and even the wheels on all of the grocery carts have obstinate minds of their own. It's important to frequent a store where the management is friendly and happy. In a business where there is happiness, there is usually quality, because the people take pride in their work.

Since food costs are a major part of our living expenses, we all need to watch for ways to save money. We can't talk about grocery shopping without mentioning redeeming coupons.

We don't save store coupons. We don't because of the small print at the bottom of them that says, "Void after_____." See, whenever we have saved coupons we've literally SAVED them. Finally, when we'd buy a new purse and throw out our old one, we'd find skeletons of yellowed and dog-eared offers at the bottom. If the old purse happened to be one of those organizer kinds with a dozen separate zippered pockets for catagorizing everything, we not only found outdated coupons we had carefully alphabetized, but all kinds of other stuff we'd given up for lost: bank book, library card, sewing kit, address book, manicure kit, and postal supplies. With so many organizing decisions to make, we'd forget which pocket we'd used for what. Once the pocket was zipped closed, the item was as good as gone.

Being organized, we have an easy, workable way to handle coupons. Recognizing their money-saving potential, we decided to enlist the help of our children.

Through the week they cut coupons from the newspaper and magazines. The coupons must be for cents off of a product we would usually buy. When the grocery list has been checked off, we go through the coupons each child has collected. If there is a coupon for an item we have on the list, it is put in an envelope with the child's name on it.

The next day at the grocery store each child takes his envelope of coupons and begins the scavenger hunt. Only your older children will be able to do this, because they will need to read the coupon to make sure they have the correct item. While most coupons say "any size," some will specify "12 oz. size," etc. Also the children will need to follow the manufacturer's requirements. Sometimes you'll have to buy two bars of soap to get the third one free. Your kids will also have to locate the items by reading the store directory. There are some rules. Once an item has been located, it must be returned to the cart before another item is found, and there is absolutely NO RUNNING!

By now you're probably wondering why the children would do this so willingly. They key to their enthusiasm is money.

We pay each child half the face value of the coupon. Figure it out.... You know any time you go to the store with your kids you're going to get ripped off for something. If they don't get you at the front door for a game of Pac-Man, they'll jump you at the cereal aisle for some Fruit Whackies or at the checkout counter for some gum. By the time you get back in the car you'll have at least fifty cents less per kid than when you got to the store. With the coupons, you split the money, so they win and so do you. They've also helped you find the things on your list, which saves time. Caution: Don't pay the money until the checker has given you cash back for the coupons. If they get their money before they've helped with the shopping, they'll be huddled in front of the cheap toy section—the place you end up in twenty minutes before a birthday party—the whole time you're in the store.

If you've organized your grocery cart neatly, the box boy will bag it that way, which will make the job of putting things away easier.

Keep all the same canned goods together so that when you get home you can unpack like items all at once. Canned goods and dry goods like sugar, flour, cat food, etc., go in the cart first because of their weight. Refrigerator items should be kept together in the basket so they will be bagged together. Frozen foods can be stacked alongside the other cold foods and should be selected last so that they don't melt.

An organized cart will speed up the checkout process, too, because the checker won't have to paw through everything to see what you've got. He won't have to ask you if you just got two cans of soup when the sale is three for a dollar.

Coming home from the store can be a nightmare if you don't have help. Expect help, ask for it, and accept it! Get help unloading, putting away, and folding sacks. Get help cleaning vegetables and organizing the refrigerator. Grocery shopping isn't easy, so no matter what... get help!

Rules to shop by:
1. Remember where you parked your car.
2. Take your list.
3. If you are a full-time homemaker, don't shop on Saturday, Sunday, or after 5 P.M. Leave those times for the homemaker who works outside her home.
4. Don't go to the store hungry.
5. Have your children help you.
6. Shop in a grocery store where the atmosphere is friendly.
7. Organize your cart as you shop.
8. Make sure your refrigerator is clean and ready for the new food.
9. Shop one day a week.
10. Don't buy soda pop unless you have your bottles to return.

10

GUESS WHO'S COMING TO DINNER—OLD MR. LEFTOVER

Leftovers have always caused problems for disorganized homemakers. We both have publicly admitted being afraid to open the Tupperware in our refrigerators for fear of what might jump out. We both have confessed that in the past, when we would store leftovers, we knew at the slam of the refrigerator door that the chances were very slim that they'd ever be seen again.

We have often wondered, but not enough to seek professional help, if we possess curious or sick minds in our ability to stand by day after day and watch the death of an eggplant. We could write, and quite scientifically, a fruit and vegetable decomposure manual. Our observation of a specimen usually starts with curiosity, then moves from intrigue to fear of picking it up with our bare hands, to disgust and, finally, to dumping it and its container.

Because sidetracked people have no concept of time, a leftover piece of meat can seem to turn overnight, when actually it has been in the refrigerator for more than three weeks. When a sidetracked person finally realizes something is wrong, it's her nose, not the calendar, that tells her.

Incidentally, sidetracked people usually have a keen sense of smell. It's probably one of the compensating factors for having the sidetracked handicap.

When leftovers inevitably turned on us, why had we bothered to go through the storing motion in the first place? How could we wrap cheese in clear plastic and then stand by and watch it disappear behind a black curtain of mold? Why did we put leftover soup in a jar, not be in the mood for it the next day, and then totally forget about it for a whole month, knowing, even though the jar was an antique glass dome and slightly violet, it would have to be thrown out? Why did we store leftovers when we ultimately knew their fate?

There were a couple of clever answers. For one thing, if the leftover remained in its serving dish, we didn't have to wash the dish. It seemed so easy to cover it up with a piece of aluminum foil and stash it in the refrigerator.

Another reason for storing was to avoid guilt. We felt terrible whenever we threw away good leftover food. If we stored it in the refrigerator until it was rotten, we were relatively guilt-free when it was obvious no one could eat it. It's very easy, almost cleansing, to throw away a head of lettuce the size of a lime. It's only right to pour pancake batter that smells like a men's locker room down the drain. Who could judge pitching green meat, yellow milk, slimy scallions, and limp carrots? Guilt-free is the homemaker who throws away a bowl of creamed soup with islands of blue fuzz on it. OR IS SHE GUILT-FREE? Not really. In fact, every time she opens her refrigerator...SHE KNOWS. Sometimes she wishes she could just get a new refrigerator.

It was obvious we had used our refrigerators and freezers as holding tanks for our guilt and as a postponing device for washing dishes. When we began to organize our kitchens we knew we had to deal with the leftover problem.

First, we decided to dump all leftovers, reasoning that the kids in India wouldn't like our cooking anyway. But our consciences wouldn't allow us to take that seriously.

Our solution to the leftover problem was so simple and so basic that we hadn't seen it. It had to begin at the store.

We would start thinking of leftovers only as another family meal. We would buy portions with that in mind. For instance, a family-size package of ten pork chops can be prepared at one time with no extra mess and then be divided into two separate meals—five chops for now and five frozen for a crisis. The family-size package is usually cheaper and allows you to build up a reserve of prepared meals you'll be grateful for when things get crazy.

On the other hand, a package with only one extra chop in it is a butcher's sneaky way to unload an extra piece of pork on the public. He knows when he weighs the package that you'll do one of three things with that extra chop:

1. eat it as you clear the table, even though you're already full;
2. give it to the dog as a reward he won't understand;
3. wrap it in foil to be balanced on top of the jar of mayonnaise and forgotten forever.

Now when we buy meats that are prewrapped, if there is too much in the package for one meal but not enough for two, we know we can ring the butcher's bell and tell him we want one end whacked off, one chop taken out, or four chops added.

When you are at the chicken counter, rummaging through the various body parts, be honest with yourself. One neck and one back left over from a fryer will make lousy soup, and two wings are not enough for a teriyaki tray.

At our house the leftovers on a fried chicken platter from a whole cut up fryer look like a Whitman Sampler after it's been around for two weeks. We don't buy a whole chicken just because that's the way it comes. Even if the price per pound is less, what's cheaper if the garbage man gets a couple of pieces?

Grocery stores today seem to be more aware of the packaging preferences of the public. There's a wider variety of separately packaged parts to choose from, and now you can buy smaller portions of larger animals. Turkey hindquarters, for example, are plentiful these days, but in our mother's day they were only available attached to the rest of the bird.

With food so fresh and plentiful and the modern conveniences of freezers and refrigerators, we can serve our families wholesome meals and stretch our budgets by eliminating waste.

The following rules for leftovers will help you achieve this goal.

Rule One: Leftovers should be double-wrapped in white freezer paper and identified by a number that corresponds to a pink 3x5 card, listing all leftover items filed in front of the divider marked "Crisis." The "Crisis" section of your card file is a list of frozen leftovers and planned-ahead meals, for the nights when you can't face the stove. We'll give you some delicious crisis recipes later (see the Appendix). There is a sample of a Crisis Card on p. 174.

Rule Two: Never serve leftovers the day after the original meal unless they can be disguised. There are a few exceptions to this rule, such as potato salad, which gets even better the next day, and meats that are just as good served cold. Our main thought was not to let our families get bored with repetition. Remember, a roast on Sunday will not be recognized when served on Monday as French dip sandwiches.

Rule Three: Buy the correct portion of food in the first place.

Rule Four: Cover properly any leftovers stored in the refrigerator, with no motive to escape washing the dish or waiting for the leftover to turn so you can throw it out.

Rule Five: Become familiar with the section in cookbooks that tells how long foods will keep. Every good cookbook has this information.

From now on you can stop thinking of leftovers as food waiting to be thrown out and start seeing them as complete meals waiting to come to your rescue.

11

PIGGING OUT

Peggy's house: 9 A.M.

We were sitting by the living room window, indulging in maple bars and washing them down with fresh hot coffee with sugar and cream. We were happy. The maple bars were baked that morning. They were so fresh that they could squish into almost nothing, like cotton candy. But halfway through the second bar we noticed that our voices had changed. We both sounded like Julia Child. We poured more coffee and continued to talk. We watched the mailman go by—Ordell's flag was up, and he didn't stop—and were tickled as she tore out of the house and ran down the street, chasing him.

Soon after, we spotted a jogger. She was pretty. Her designer running wear was probably a size eight.

"I want to look like that."

"Do you want to start jogging?"

"No, but I want an outfit like hers."

"You can't have one."

"Why?"

"Because you'll sleep in it and you'll never jog."

"How do you know?"

"Because you hate to sweat."

"So?"

"So, if you run, you'll sweat."

"So I'll get the suit anyway."

"It won't be right. It won't look the same."

"Why?"

"It'll be a size fourteen."

Neither of us liked to sweat. The thought of rigorous exercise took both of us back to the agony of high school phys ed. We loved to be comfortable and, since it's obvious that strenuous exercise is not comfortable, we had given it up for a more sedentary life. Unfortunately, the effects of an inactive life were noticeable in some obvious places. Our backs got fat. Sidesaddles had developed, giving us a resemblance to English equestriennes. Like sand castles, our bodies were beginning to display grapelike clusters here and there. We were ashamed of ourselves. Pleased with our bust measurements while bending over, we found that somehow the impressive dimensions disappeared when we stood up. We blamed it on gravity. We tried to blame the condition of our bodies on anything but lack of exercise and too much food.

What should we do? We envied women our age who were still in good shape. How did they have the self-discipline to deny themselves mayonnaise, chocolate, real butter, and sugar? How could they be satisfied with imitations? We admired their ability to stick to an exercise routine.

It's a good thing that jogging suits were not in style when we were slobs. Embarrassment was one of the key motivations to change back in 1977. In our slob days we often had to answer the door in our nightgowns at three in the afternoon. We'd say we were recuperating from an illness. If jogging suits had been available then, we would have bought them in several colors. Makers claim that they are extremely comfortable for running, but that same comfort can be applied to sleeping, and sleeping would have been what we would have done in them. Then if someone had come to the door at three in the afternoon, we'd have been caught in our jogging suits, not our nightgowns.

Caught in a jogging suit? Hardly.

4 P.M.

"Hi. I'm sorry I didn't call before I came over. Just on a whim I thought I'd drop by and—oh, I see I've caught you when you're exercising."

"Oh, that's okay. I was just getting ready to jog. Let's go sit on the front porch."

The more hours we would have spent in the suits, the more athletic we would have looked. In fact, we would have looked like marathoners.

We've said this before, but it bears repeating. Sidetracked people generally have a lot of energy but lack direction. So food in the hands of a Sidetracked Home Executive™ can be fattening. Disorganized people notoriously end up at the refrigerator door for lack of knowing what else to do or where else to go. Without direction, they will unconsciously pack away handfuls of chocolate chips while making the cookie dough, and spoonfuls of butter-cream frosting while icing a cake.

While clearing the table after a meal, they finish what's left on each person's place. Because of the frequent interruptions that make sitting down to a hot meal almost impossible, they have developed an indiscriminating taste for cold food. Unfortunately, all these unconscious snacking patterns eventually show up on the hips.

Through our experiences with food, we knew that after all our years of sidetracked food preparation, we would have to diet.

Just as we'd read all the books on how to get organized and they hadn't helped us, we'd tried all the latest diet programs and they hadn't worked either. Diets are based on keeping track of yourself. It was easy to see why all the dieting we'd tried in our slob days was in vain.

Now that we had our kitchens organized, we were prepared to lose weight.

From Peggy:

My resolution to lose weight was aided by the fact that I

had to have some corrective jaw surgery and for the six-week recovery period my mouth would be wired shut. I learned a lot about myself through that experience, and because of it I was able to acquire some better eating habits.

I found out that my tongue is like an anteater's when it comes to getting the last bit of jelly off a table knife after making peanut butter and jelly sandwiches. Usually quick and thorough, my tongue couldn't do its work because it was locked behind rows of teeth. Still the reflex action was there for twenty-one days, so every afternoon it was my custom to make lunch for the kids and then smear jelly across my teeth with the knife.

I found out that I would habitually leave generous amounts of whatever I cooked on the utensils, specifically for licking purposes. Potato salad, chocolate frosting, and whipped cream were my favorites. I used to wonder why a recipe that said "serves six" never did. Now I know it was because I'd eat at least two of the servings as I cooked, and I never counted the calories I'd consumed before sitting down to a meal. I considered them merely a part of the clean-up process. While preparing meals I used to lick knives, beaters, and bowls at laser speed. It took only crashing a beater twenty-one times into my clenched teeth before I stopped the involuntary reaction.

I can attribute at least six pounds of my weight loss to the fact that my tongue was imprisoned for more than twenty-one days.

I watched people gorge themselves with food as I sipped my meager meals through a straw.

I lost my knack for conversation. Obsessed with the thought of food, I couldn't contribute intelligently to any serious discussion. The Falklands dispute made me crave tacos. Even a newsbreak brought hunger pangs. If I heard "Fire rages through national forest . . . film at eleven," I'd mentally roast a Ball Park frank. Songs made me hungry if they mentioned food. If I heard "God didn't make little green apples . . ." on the radio, I yearned for hot apple pie. But TV was the worst. On every channel there was someone chomping

down on a Big Mac and fries or two hands breaking apart a
steaming Chicken McNugget.

I sadistically read detailed recipes in magazines for barbecued ribs and lobster Newburg. I drooled over the pictures
and suffered the pain of full color.

After the third week I seemed to transcend the cravings
and had become aloof. As an observer, I recognized myself
as I witnessed gluttony. Everyone ate too fast. At salad bars
people piled their plates beyond reason. In theaters they
bought tubs of buttered popcorn to devour in the dark. At
the pizza parlor I watched a couple order the giant
combination. I saw people walk away with sagging paper
plates at a church potluck, and at a Sunday brunch I
counted the times the same bulging green pantsuit attacked
the chocolate mousse. I wanted to educate everyone on
overindulgence. I wanted them to realize that all they really
wanted was to satisfy a taste. If everyone could be wired
shut for at least twenty-one days, they would see the truth
of appetite.

The words "just a taste" kept going through my mind. "If
I could have just a taste of fresh strawberries, a taste of
Kentucky Fried Chicken, a taste of a T-bone steak...I won't
abuse my eating ability."

I can open my mouth now, but I haven't forgotten the rule
of just a taste and I haven't gained an ounce. I'm eating
"just a taste" of everything I want. It feels so good to be a
size seven instead of being limited to solid black, or vertical
stripes. I can wear whatever I like. Now when we go out to
dinner my husband says, "Is that all you can eat, babe?"
instead of "Boy, I can't believe you ate that whole thing."

From Pam:

I knew that Peggy would be twenty pounds lighter after
being "wired" for six weeks, and I wasn't about to let her
get thin and lovely alone. On the day of her surgery I
decided to lose weight, too. My only other choice was to
sneak into my sister's hospital room and periodically add
Wesson oil to her IV.

In the days that followed my decision to reduce, I was

dismayed at what I had to go through. There were so many
side effects. I learned that my usual caloric intake had far
exceeded the U.S. Recommended Daily Allowance for
homemakers. I made that discovery by consuming only
1,200 calories per day. I felt deprived. I was disgusted to
find out that my happiness depended on the level of starches
and animal fat in my system.

I was starving, unhappy, cranky, and unpredictable. I felt
cheated whenever I saw someone eating ice cream. I had
technicolor buffet dreams. I lost all of my joy for living. I
was a martyr. Everyone unfortunate enough to come close
to me got a detailed report of what I had eaten so far that
day. I hadn't learned to diet in silence. I was arrogant and
boastful if I'd lost a pound, and when someone asked me
how much I had lost, I lied.

The test of suffering had left is mark. I wrote a dieter's
prayer in an effort to be both strong in will and humble in
my response to compliments. I prayed:

Oh, dear God,
Give me this day my daily bread,
even though I'll have to cut the crusts off.
Help me to eat it without butter
and blackberry jelly spread all over it.
Forgive me for coveting the food on the
plates of others. Guide me away
from the bakery section at Mark 'n Buy.
Keep me steadfast in the fruit and produce
section. Help me to know the glory
of good nutrition. Let me find contentment
and satisfaction in a medley of mustard greens
(1/2 cup, boiled, drained—16 calories),
three leaves of Romaine lettuce
(8" long, sprinkled with lemon juice—8 calories),
and a cup of bouillon (5 calories).
Lead me not near the doorways to Mrs. See's or
Dunkin' Donuts,
and deliver me from the desire

to bake a batch of chocolate chip cookies
just so I can eat the dough.
Please take my sweet tooth and
give it to Bernice Jordan, who only
weighs 106 pounds.
Forgive me for acting
smart-alecky around Doretta June.
Lord, you know better than I that
with a few more banana splits I'd be in her shoes.
I ask these things so that my body might be a testimony to
your loving and nourishing support rather than
my misuse of your abundance.
Thank you, Father.
Amen.

When my prayer was finished I was soothed until a group of negative fat cells assaulted my faith. Defiantly they presented their case. Momentarily I sided with their logic and turned on my sister. I thought, *Sure, it's easy for her to resolve to lose weight; she can't open her mouth. Here I am in the real world.* If you sit and think too long about how unfair things are, you'll get stuck in your own self-pity.

A week passed and I was still listening to the arguments. In the meantime Richard Simmons was begging me to get off my cellulite, and Peggy had lost four pounds.

I was getting panicky. I had to move. I joined a beginners' aerobics class, not realizing how out of condition I was. The first few lessions were excruciating and I had to go to bed early, but the extreme torture I experienced was a sign that I was serious about losing weight.

The prayer began to take hold, and dieting and exercise got easier. Within six weeks I had lost ten pounds. Peggy and I went shopping for summer clothes. For the first time since our last babies we made our selection from the petite rack.

If you are overweight as we were, you'll find that getting your kitchen organized will be the first step toward losing weight permanently. You will be able to stay on any reasonable weight-loss program and exercise routine because you will be in control of your menus, grocery shopping, and meal preparation.

Your body will be a testimony to God's nourishing support, and you will be satisfied with just a taste of everything you love.

12

THE HARVEST MARTYR

Ring...ring...ring...

"Hello."

"Hi. Do you want to go over to the Can Can with me and put up a few batches of carrots?"

"What's the Can Can?"

"It's a place where you take the stuff you've picked, and they clean it and can it for you."

"You want to take a bunch of carrots over there? Why? You hate canned carrots."

"I know, but it's the only thing that's left to can this season. Come on, go with me, please?"

"Sissy, what's the matter with you?"

"Oh, I'm so depressed. I just came from Nancy's. You should see her pantry!"

"What's it like?"

"It's just like the picture in that book Mom has."

"What book?"

"You know, *Planting, Pruning, Picking, Peeling, Pitting and Packing: The Encyclopedia of Food Preservation.*"

"I hate that book. It makes me feel guilty."

"Me, too."

"They want you to feel guilty. They know we all have some of that pioneer spirit in us, and they use that to sell books."

(The last time we'd gotten the urge to can something it had cost us $873. We bought several cases of those cute bicentennial jars, one of those huge blue-speckled porcelain canners, a pressure cooker, a freezer, a Seal-a-Sack, a couple of twenty-five-pound bags of sugar, six dozen plastic-coated freezer cartons, not to mention the mini-tiller and the branch-whacker. And all we made that year was strawberry jam.)

"What's wrong with us? I don't even want to plant a garden."

"I don't either. It's a big commitment. Once everything starts coming up, you've got to do something with it."

"I know. I let the plum tree get away from me this year, and I really feel guilty about it."

"You're kidding. The plums are gone? It seems like it was just yesterday you were yelling at the kids not to eat them because they were green."

"I know, and now Danny's out mowing the lawn and pits are flying everywhere. It's such a waste."

"Oh, Peg, don't be so ashamed. Have you seen your birds lately?"

"What about them?"

"You've got the fattest, happiest birds anywhere."

"I do?"

"Yeah. They're full of plums!"

"That's true. The other day I woke up and the whole tree was shaking."

"See? Think how grateful they are."

"Come to think of it, I haven't seen a single bird in Ordell's yard this year."

"I can believe that."

"Last year she won mason jar's Wide-Mouth Woman of the Year award."

"I can believe that, too!"

Ordell worked full-time at the local cannery, sorting

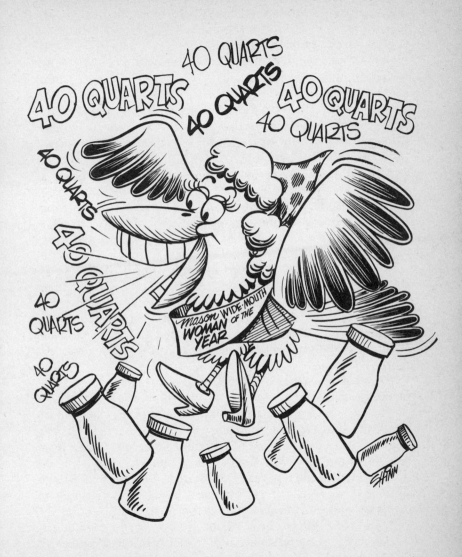

snakes out of the green beans, and still came home and met the canning needs of her family. She wore a white hairnet and support stockings from June through November. We had heard that she moved, emotionless, from fruit to fruit, following the crops.

"She'd like me to come for coffee sometime and bring my sister."

"I don't want to go!"

"Me, either. If I have to hear one more time how she was up all night with her Bartletts, I'll scream. She called me this morning with a quart count."

"How many did she do?"

"Fifty."

"And you watch, those jars will be out on the counter until Christmas, when she'll have to make room for her baked goods for holiday gift-giving."

"She's such a boast-honker."

"A boast-honker?"

"Yeah, I made it up, but don't you think it fits?"

"I think you're jealous."

"Me, jealous of a wide-mouth boast-honker?"

We were envious that she took advantage of the bounty of nature while we let nature take advantage of us. Ordell was like a mother squirrel with her nest full of nuts, ready for winter.

"I want the feeling that Ordell must have, now that everything's done."

"Okay, we want that feeling, but it's too late to do anything about it this year; everything's already gone. How about if we buy a bunch of different jams and jellies from the store and soak off the labels. Then we could put on those cute little labels that say 'From the Kitchen of So and So.'"

"It wouldn't be the same. I love the smell of jelly cooking."

"I do, too. Okay, how about if, during the delabeling process, we put a tablespoon of Welch's in the vaporizer?"

"Yeah, and out on the counter we'll have a set of tongs, a package of pectin, and a bar of paraffin."

"Okay, and we'll wear aprons."

"Yeah, and we'll make just enough of a mess to feel like we really did something!"

It was wonderful. The aroma of jelly permeated the entire house. We couldn't resist inviting Ordell over to inspect our newly relabeled jars. Her mouth dropped open; her rough, purple-stained hands fell to her sides. The variety was incredible: grape, blackberry, red raspberry, currant, plum, boysenberry, mixed fruit, blueberry, peach, apricot, orange marmalade, and apple butter. True, we only had two jars of each flavor, but Ordell evidently assumed we had charitably given the extras to those less fortunate than we.

Ordell had a way of making you want to get even, but the bottom line was, we wished we had her pantry. There had to be a middle of the road. We didn't want to commit our entire lives to gardens and quart jars, but we wanted to be a part of the glory of creation, when God uses man to complete His plan.

There is something very spiritual about planting a garden. It is almost like saying to God, "Yes, I will take Your seedlings into my care. I promise to raise them to please You." We'd already promised to do that with six of His human babies. Now were we ready to venture into the wonderful world of His plants? Had we done a good enough job with His children? The answer, of course, was yes!

We would make mistakes, as gardeners do, but He must have known that, or He wouldn't have entrusted us with the earth and a package of seeds. Evidently He was willing to take the risk with us. After all, nothing planted, nothing grown. We had to disregard the awesomeness of the responsibility and go for it!

We armed ourselves with shovels, rakes, hoes, seeds, and the willingness to devote our time and energy to roots instead of prenatal vitamins; to fertilizer instead of diapers; to tillers and weed-whackers instead of playpens and vaporizers. We would spend our time reading what the plant doctor had to say, just as we had memorized Dr. Dobson's every word. We would pull the weeds away from each of God's sprouts, just as we had protected our children against violence and sex on television. We would cultivate the soil all around each plant, just as we had cultivated the principles of laughter, love, and peace in our homes.

We were cautious during the next growing season not to overcompensate for the years gone by. We decided to start small, with a little garden patch rather than trying to compete with Ordell's north forty. We figured if we were successful on a small scale, we would consider enlarging our garden the next year.

It would be dumb to invest a lot of money in farm equipment and plow up the entire backyard until we had proved to ourselves that we could take care of a small patch from start to finish. We had failed before, as one of our youngest reminded us.

"Boy, Aunt Peg, I sure hope we can keep track of this stuff after working so hard to get it planted."

"Keep track of it?"

"Yeah. We'll have to remember to water it and then pick it when it's done."

"We won't forget. We're organized now!"

"I hope so. . . . When we lived at the house with the dead pear trees, my mom planted one of these and forgot all about it."

"She did?"

"Yeah, and then one day when it was time to eat dinner, she said to me, 'Joanna, go out and see if there's any corn on the cob,' and I did, but there was only one and it was brown and slimy."

This time we chose an inconspicuous spot, lest the seeds fail to do what the packages said they'd do and the whole mess become an eyesore to neighbors and passersby. One of us found an unused area behind the garage—the dimensions of a king-size bed—where tall rows of golden corn would hide the heat pump. The other made use of a county easement at the border of her property, where twenty-five feet of garden hose could reach easily for water.

Since we were both insecure about farming, we decided to consult an expert; we called Nancy. She has the rare quality of knowing what she's doing without holding it over the heads of those of us who don't. It was early spring and she had marked her acre to be planted and bordered it with flowering plants. We thought it was another case like the wallpaper in the chicken coop, but she explained that bugs would be attracted to the flowers instead of the vegetables. It made sense; besides, it was pretty.

Nancy warned us only to plant the things we loved and to beware of impulse buying, spurred by the unrealistic fluorescent-colored pictures on the front of the seed packages. She advised us to steer clear of peanuts, bananas, coconuts, pineapples, sugarcane, and papaya, since we live in the Northwest, warning that crops not suited to the climate should be bought ready-grown.

She also cautioned that the seeds in the standard envelopes, displayed on turntables nationwide, would be too generous for our small garden sizes. We were to dispose of the extra seeds, since they would lose their freshness and potency and wouldn't be good the following year. We are born savers, so throwing anything away is hard to do. We were faced with a real dilemma. Should we create a co-op in our community, called Share-a-Seed? Should we use the mini-tiller and wipe out a large swath of lawn to accommodate the extra seeds, or should we toss them over the hill and let nature take its course?

We liked the idea of sharing the seeds, but we didn't want to get involved with running a co-op, Robert's Rules of Order, treasury reports, new business, old business, car pools, mailing lists, or potlucks.

We decided to go seed shopping together. The packages told how far the seeds would go, so it was obvious how many to buy. Some of the things we wanted to eat, such as tomatoes, broccoli, brussels sprouts, cabbage, cauliflower, and eggplant, were already teenage plants, available in plastic containers. We had the choice of going that route or starting from scratch. Sidetracked people need to think very carefully before starting anything from scratch. Their intentions are always so good but rarely materialize into a finished product. Besides, it was too late for us to start with seeds; they'd be ready to transplant on Halloween.

Ordell had a greenhouse the size of a gymnasium in her

backyard. She had planted her seeds one cold, snowy day while we made snowmen and drank cocoa. We would have to compensate for playing while Ordell had sown. A plastic container with eight cabbage plants cost us fifty-nine cents. A fifty-nine-cent package of seeds, sprouted first in a hothouse, then transplanted to the garden, would yield a fifty-foot row of cabbages. But since the kids cried every time we served cabbage in any form, we were satisfied to buy the eight plants in the plastic container for fifty-nine cents and split them between us. Four plants would be enough for each of us to meet her family's cabbage requirements. More important, Ordell couldn't buy our memories of playing in the snow with the kids and coming in for hot cocoa and dry mittens. And fifty-nine cents seemed a small price to pay for those memories.

Before you plan to break into the wonderful world of agriculture, read these rules.

30 RULES TO GROW BY

1. Get your ground ready during the first nice weather.
2. Make sure your dirt is clear of rocks, bricks, tin cans, Popsicle sticks, gum wrappers, apple cores, dog bones, and *Star Wars* action figures.
3. Don't buy impulsively at the seed counter.
4. Start small.
5. Plant only things the family loves.
6. Plant at least two "ego crops," like radishes and green beans.
7. Never plant alone. Get your family to help.
8. If you plan to travel, don't plant at all.
9. Buy and wear garden gloves.
10. Make friends with a farmer.
11. Borrow the farmer's tools.
12. Space your rows to correspond to your shoe size (allowing for your plants' natural maturity).
13. Don't plant wallflowers next to hog plants. Example: green onions next to pumpkins.
14. If this is your first garden, don't plant for profit.

15. If you can't take care of your house plants, don't plant a garden.
16. Don't grow to impress. In other words, don't flaunt your crop.
17. Don't save leftover seeds.
18. If it doesn't rain, water.
19. If it rains, don't water.
20. Be patient. (Don't pull up carrots to see how they're progressing.)
21. Keep rabbits, squirrels, possums, and birds away from your garden by using a scarecrow or papier-mâché cats.
22. Keep deer away by tying your teenager to a post outside your garden when he's been grounded.
23. Keep toddlers away from the garden if they eat dirt.
24. Plan to spend ten minutes per day in the garden for each king-size-bed space.
25. Always remember, Mr. Worm is your friend and he won't bite.
26. Don't feel embarrassed if you have to go to the produce section of your grocery store.
27. A garden planted too late will attract flies.
28. Don't expect the harvest to look like the seed package.
29. Don't reap on an empty stomach.
30. Weed with wisdom. (Know your plants.)

13

SIDETRACKED AND SINGLE

From Pam:
Somehow in my life I have always attracted free food. My husband was a sales representative for a large food company for the first seven years of our marriage, and the manager of a fast-food restaurant for the remaining seven years. As a salesman it was his job to service grocery stores, stock the shelves with new products, and remove any damaged or outdated goods. Other salesmen with the same job, but different products, would trade their spoils for ours in the grocery store parking lots.

"Hi, guy... how goes it?"

"Can't complain. How about you?"

"Oh, fair to middlin'. You got any spoils?"

"Yeah. How are you fixed for cereal?"

"I got Choo Choo Treats and Oatmobiles. Pick your poison."

"What's the date on the Oatmobiles?"

"They're only two months over their shelf life."

"Great! Hey, there's the cheese rep. Hi, Jack. You workin' hard or hardly workin'?"

"Oh, I'm stayin' out of trouble. You guys need any cheese?"

During those years my husband kept the pantry full. The food was free; it wasn't fresh, but it was still welcomed. Every consumable thing in our home was the result of bartering, and grocery shopping was almost unnecessary. Later we became the owners of a fast-food restaurant. The food kept coming except that now it was prepared and served. I was allowed to bring the children in regularly. With the restaurant open twenty-four hours, seven days a week, meal-planning was unnecessary. If somebody wanted chicken and somebody wanted fish, it wasn't my problem. The restaurant's menu was diversified enough to please everyone's appetite.

I divorced after fourteen years of marriage and spent the next two years eating at Peggy's house. Those two years at my sister's were not intentional. I unconsciously found myself and my three children at her doorstep every evening around 5:30. It wasn't until the second anniversary of my divorce that I realized I hadn't unpacked my cooking utensils.

"Sissy, you wrote a check to Pay 'n Takit for two hundred sixty dollars? How long will that much food last?"

"Well, I go every Tuesday."

"You spend two hundred sixty dollars every week on food?"

"Yeah, about that much."

"You've got five people, and I've got four. You've only got one more person in your family than I do and I only spend forty dollars a week. How come you spend so much more than I do?"

"I don't know. With nine people for dinner every night, I guess it adds up."

"Am I here every night?"

"No, not every night. You eat at Mom's some of the time."

It was painfully clear to me that I had become a moocher. It was true, but somehow the thought of cooking for myself and my children left something to be desired . . . a man. I love to cook for a man. I love to have guests for dinner and have the man ask for seconds. I love the coffee commercial where she doesn't think he'll have more and he does! I love it when a man doesn't leave room for dessert but has it anyway. There's no higher compliment than for a man to have to undo his belt and crawl to the living room.

I don't think it was an apple that Eve got Adam to bite; it was an apple pie. And I think Adam knew it would hurt her feelings if he didn't eat it. Adam and Eve started the whole order of things. That's why, when we were little, Peggy and I made mud pies while Kenny Hathaway was making mud bombs. While he built up an arsenal, we set the table. Kenny was the first man we ever served, and he was beguiled by our domestic creativity. Growing up, we watched Dad rave over a wonderful meal and heard Grandpa say to Granny, "How 'bout fixin' me somethin' good to eat, Ma?" She always did.

Any menu I ever planned had a man in mind. I knew Gloria Steinem would be appalled and disgusted. She'd hate to hear me say, "He's not here, so we'll just heat a can of Campbell's Chunky." I knew I'd never be a subservient Edith Bunker, but I couldn't deny wanting to show off my culinary wizardry to gain praise and adoration from a man. After all, the way to a man's heart is through his taste buds. I talked to Peggy about it.

"Sissy, do you think it's wrong to want to cook for a man?"

"Huh?"

"I mean... do you want to cook when Danny's on swing shift?"

"Not really. I usually just heat up a can of Chunky Soup and we eat some sandwiches."

"See. We cook for men!"

"We do?"

"Yeah, and it's all Adam and Eve's fault."

"Huh?"

"Oh, never mind."

"Sissy, what are you talking about?"

"I just realized that I want to cook for men, and if there

isn't one around . . . I don't want to make the effort. I wish I was more like Miss Salter."

"Who's Miss Salter?"

"You know, my high school English teacher."

Miss Salter was an inspiration. A small woman, in excellent physical condition, she was strikingly attractive. She was in her late forties and had never married. On one occasion, years after graduation, I dropped by her apartment unexpectedly. It was about 6:30 in the evening. She answered the door in a long, graceful black-and-white caftan. Assuming she was expecting company, I apologized for my impulsive visit and said I would come back some other time. She asked me in, assuring me that no one was coming. I smelled a roast in the oven. Candles flickered. Gershwin's *Rhapsody in Blue* came from somewhere. She invited me to join her with a glass of wine. Following her to the dining room, I marveled at the lovely table she had set. There was a single china plate with a dainty cup and saucer on a pale blue linen cloth with a matching napkin.

Miss Salter had always made the dinner hour something special. She told me that she had decided years ago that the quality of her meals could not depend on whether or not she shared them with a man. She treated herself to the best. Instead of eating, she dined.

If I had never married and was in my late forties, someone dropping by my apartment around 6:30 would have found a short, fat, bitter woman in a repulsive knee-length yellow mumu and thongs. The aroma of fresh popcorn—dinner—would have greeted the guest and invaded the entire complex. *Gilligan's Island* blaring in the background would have made conversation impossible. No candles, no china, no linen . . . just wine.

Eating is a very social activity. I have always felt that food is meant to be shared, otherwise chickens would have only one drumstick. Our culture makes the sharing of food almost a ceremony. When I'd go to a restaurant and see a person alone at a table for two, I thought it looked pitiful. A person might be in town to buy Twentieth Century–Fox, but if she eats alone in a restaurant, she looks like a loser. She could also look like a lush. Champagne raised in a toast between two people looks marvelous. If the couple happens to be a man and woman, it looks terribly romantic. If the people are the same sex, they look successful, no doubt toasting the consummation of a big business deal. A single person, sipping alone, looks like a probable drunk.

I had to eat in a restaurant alone on two occasions and, because of my insecurity as a single woman, it was an awful experience.

I did several things to look productive, vital, and self-content until my food came. I kept looking toward the lobby as if waiting for someone. I checked my watch, pretending to be concerned and showing a progressive agitation as time passed. I snapped my fingers as if I had just thought of something important, then quickly scribbled on a napkin. I dropped something. I picked fuzz off myself. With a sudden look of urgency, I began frantically looking through my purse and pockets. I went through my keys one by one, silently quizzing myself as to what they fit.

I read the place mat and memorized the story of how the restaurant began. I listed a long column of numbers on my napkin, then took out my calculator and added up the figures. I looked pleased with the total. I rearranged the table. I read the information on a packet of Sweet 'n Low. I chuckled to myself, making everyone else in the restaurant feel left out. I stared out the window as if in deep contemplation of a pending decision. Finally my food came. Miss Salter had learned something that I hadn't: how to eat alone and not feel sorry for herself.

You can also feel sorry for yourself when you're single and you come home to a dark house and a cold, empty oven. You open the front door and the house smells like the Evergreen Hotel—closed for restoration. You know you belong there but you wish you didn't. For a moment you stand still while one of the kids trips over the cat and snaps on the light. The house is chilly; everyone is starving and you're exhausted. A smothering sense of self-pity comes from the fact that you've worked hard all day and the evening's just begun.

For all the years that Ozzie came home to Harriet, candles, and a hot oven, I wonder if he really appreciated it.

Recently I had a chance to see what it would be like to be the head of the Nelson family. Peggy and I have an office three miles from our homes. During an exceptionally busy time, it was necessary for one of us to keep working until around 6 P.M. (We normally close at 3 P.M.) Peggy offered to pick up all six kids and fix dinner at her house. Knowing that everything was under control, I could relax and focus all of my attention on business. As I locked up the office at 6:15 I was numb from making decisions. I was sick of my own voice, let alone anyone else's, and I was physically drained. I was so thankful to be going home to Peggy's house instead of the Evergreen Hotel.

There were lights and I could hear children's laughter, but it wasn't the fiendish kind that comes with lack of food. Somebody was monkeying with the stereo; somebody was scolding the puppy; somebody was practicing the piano; but the noise didn't matter because dinner was ready and everybody knew it.

When I came through the door, my kids ran to greet me. The house was warm, the table was set, and a delicious dinner was waiting for me.

When I left Peggy's house that night I did a lot of thinking on the way home. I realized that I could create that same scenario for myself in my own home.

I could have the table set if, in the morning when the kids unloaded the dishwasher, they put the plates, glasses, and silverware on the table instead of back into the cupboard. I could have lights on if I plugged in one of those automatic light-turner-oners that people use when they go on vacation. I could turn the thermostat up a bit (not so much as to be an energy hog, but just enough to take the chill off the house). By using the "Timed Bake" button and my Crock-Pot, I could be greeted by the aroma of a wonderful meal. It occurred to me that self-pity is brought on by fatigue, but to do these things for myself and my family in the morning would give me a feeling of superiority.

The desire to cook for a man and the distaste for eating alone clearly were two problems I still had to solve. Dee Anne helped me, too. Dee Anne is a close friend of Peggy's and mine. She has helped us in our business as well as our personal lives. If you read our first book, you'll find her in our acknowledgments. I love her dearly. She won't know that this story she told me changed my life until she reads this page.

Dee Anne is married to Dan, and they have two small boys. She is a born organized person but has the unique capacity to understand sidetracked people. Her meals are planned carefully and prepared and served on time...always. She told us that one evening she fixed a special meal that was planned to knock Dan's socks off. She cooks for men, too. She even fixed his favorite dessert—apple Betty. I don't remember what the special occasion was but, knowing Dee Anne, there might not even have been one.

When it was time to serve this scrumptious meal, she called everyone to the table. You can imagine how perfect it looked. The little ones came running, eager to eat. Dan was nowhere to be seen.

She found him downstairs, asleep on the sofa and full of potato chips and dip. She nudged him gently and told him dinner was ready. He said, "Honey, I'm sorta full. You guys go ahead and eat without me. Can you just put mine on hold?"

She was furious, charged upstairs in a rage, stuffed the Betty down the garbage disposal, and sat down to the table with the kids.

They could see how upset she was. Their attempts at helping her feel better are what cleared me of my error in thinking. Dee Anne told Peggy and me that one of the boys said, as if he were reading a script, "Wow, Mom, this is a great dinner!" The other one chimed in, "I love the way you cook your beans!" She said she looked into their bright little eyes and realized they were just as important as Dan.

I've been single now for four years and the men I've met,

who live alone, have taught me another lesson: that men are just as competent with pots and pans as women are. A man who has learned how to cook for himself makes a wonderful date. He'll give you recipes and household tips, derived from desperation, and another point of view. He'll be grateful to taste your cooking and will help with the dishes, expecting nothing in return. He is usually thrown into an empty kitchen without even the benefit of Miss Cratsberry. If he is used to having a woman do everything for him, he's shocked at the scope of responsibility.

I've never missed a chance to drag good ideas from any willing male who has a creative mind. One man bragged, "To save time and mess in the kitchen at meal time, I eat over the sink." Another man said since he was eating out so much, he decided to remodel the kitchen and turn it into an extra bedroom. One very inventive gentleman explained, "I always keep a supply of frozen hamburger patties on hand. Even though I may never use them, I feel secure knowing they are there." That same man told me it was mandatory to talk your kids into buying school lunches. . . . So wise.

Between Miss Salter, Peggy, Dee Anne, and the men I've met, I have completely changed my attitude about preparing meals. It has really helped me to implement our new system for organizing my kitchen; but in addition to that, I've found that I'm cooking with more love.

I have become aware of three very important gifts that have been given to me by God: the sense of taste and smell, and an appetite. I have taken these three gifts for granted all my life. We usually don't appreciate things until we lose them. I lost my senses of taste and smell once when I had a bad cold and I burnt my tongue on a cup of cocoa. I guess, because it was temporary, I didn't reflect on it very much. I've lost my appetite many times, usually when I get nervous or worried. I do remember how the joy of eating was gone without taste and smell.

Think about the pleasures of taste and smell. They aren't dependent on whether or not you eat with somebody. And appetite—what an incredible thing. It is responsible for keeping us alive; it gives us the desire to eat. When our children are sick, we know they are on the road to recovery when they say, "I'm hungry!" I love to hear those words after one of my kids has had a bout with a fever.

With my new attitude I definitely have more joy! I cook with love, and I have a thankfulness and appreciation for good food and its abundance in my life. Do I still cook for men? Yes...but I think that's okay, because I cook for myself and my children, too.

14

TROUBLE AT THE TROUGH

From Peggy:

The greatest problem American families face today isn't crime, drug abuse, nuclear warfare, or inflation. It's eating in front of the TV. Mealtime is the main opportunity for togetherness, but the invasion of the tube has slowly eroded most family communication.

I used to think it was the TV's fault that we rarely sat down to the table together, but then I remembered that I had grown up with television in my childhood home. As a rule, though, my sister and I ate with our parents in the dining room, with matching plates and cloth napkins—no TV.

I also remembered that we didn't get our set—a twenty-one-inch, black-and-white Packard Bell, Early American console—until 1954. Mom and Dad had been on a regular eating schedule since they got married in 1940, and Mom had had many years to get organized before the invention of television.

The day the TV arrived at our house we spent the entire afternoon glued to Channel 12 (the only one in operation), but when dinner was ready at the usual time, we turned off the set and moved to the dining room. We hurried to finish dinner, clear the table, and do the dishes in time to watch Ozzie and Harriet eat. The television was for special occasions, instead of a constant companion.

There was always laughter and sharing at mealtime, but no TV. Mom always served meals on time and, once she took off her apron and sat down, she never needed to return to the kitchen for forgotten items. We were sent off to school well fed and happy. At the end of the day we'd come back down the long driveway and smell the beginnings of a wonderful meal. We knew Mom would be there and the table would be set for dinner, with fresh-cut flowers from the garden as the centerpiece.

We were reared like TV's David and Ricky. Not that we didn't know what our dad did for a living, but our home looked like the combined sets of *Ozzie and Harriet, The Donna Reed Show, Leave It to Beaver,* and *Father Knows Best.* In fact, if we'd been boys, our names probably would have been David and Beaver.

I cherished those wonderful memories and, because they were so happy, I wanted to duplicate them in my own home. Unfortunately, the TV tray and the tract house ruined my plans. The mobility and convenience of those trays and the proximity of the family room to the eating area in a typical tract house have changed the course of American history. We found ourselves eating frozen dinners in front of the TV.

If I could have gone straight from the altar to the dining room table, I could have set the precedent for where my family would eat. But sidetracked by the romance of the honeymoon, I let the chance to set a precedent pass me by. When I got married I found myself thrust into a vacant apartment with a black-and-white portable, rabbit ears, and two TV trays. I was delighted to find that those frozen, synthetic convenience foods, in divided containers, fit neatly onto the TV trays we'd been given as wedding gifts. I soon discovered that my husband would unconsciously eat anything I put on his tray while he watched his favorite shows. With the birth of each child I'd cash in my Green Stamps at the local redemption center and add more trays to the collection. By 1976 we had acquired the complete, deluxe nature series (enough scenic-patterned trays to entertain and feed six additional couples).

I also blame today's architects for designing the tract house and thereby affecting the quality of the American family's dining experience. When they created the tract house, they added the extra bathroom off the master bedroom, but they eliminated the dining room, replacing it with a small space off the kitchen, called the eating area. The plastic chandelier hanging over this space served two purposes. It marked the spot where you should put your dinette set, and it divided the family room—with the TV—from the kitchen. This mass-produced house plan, coupled with the invention of the TV tray, eliminated the need for a dinette set. But furniture manufacturers quickly pointed out that the clearance level of the average adult male is more than five feet. Once again the dinette set was necessary if a clumsy husband wanted to avoid multiple contusions from swinging plastic crystal.

In my slob days I used the dinette set for craft projects while I watched TV, and I was grateful not to have to clear it in order to eat. We ate on the trays. When I got organized I converted the extra bedroom—junk room—into the sewing and crafts room, which left the dinette set bare for the first time in years.

With my table clear and time invested in planning menus, shopping for groceries, and preparing food to perfection, I wanted meals to be enjoyed and appreciated. It was time for a change. After all my effort I wasn't willing to let my dinette set become a huge TV tray, but I didn't want my family to rebel during the transition from tray to table.

How do you tell someone who is grafted to the aluminum legs of a TV tray that he must now get up and walk to the dinette set?

"Come on, everybody.... Dinner's ready!"

"It's my turn to use the Big Bird tray."

"It is not. You had it last night."

"Mom...how come I always get stuck with Mount Saint Helens? It's crooked!"

"Hey, babe, hand me my Dolly Parton tray."

"We don't need the trays tonight. We all get to eat at the table."

"Huh?"

"Where?"

"Come on. I've got it all set. Turn off the TV."

"Huh?"

"What?"

"Say what?"

"I said, dinner is ready and we're gonna eat at the table."

"Where's the portable, Dad?"

"I'll get it. You guys go sit down."

The table was lovingly set for a wonderful family time together—and the appearance of a ten-inch color portable TV as a centerpiece was disgusting. I had to make a decision, and it was clear to me that there were two choices: The television would remain on, or it would be turned off. The ramifications of either choice also were very clear. If the TV was turned off, it would blow the possibility of having any pleasant family conversation. Everybody but me would eat in hostile silence. But if the TV remained on, I would experience the hot, purple, intense hate that accompanies revolution.

Considering the marriage, I decided to leave the TV on for the time being and, more important, to hold my anger until after the meal. Through many years of wedded bliss I had discovered that the best way to fight was in the *past tense*, after the hot, purple rage had diminished and I could fight with facts instead of tears and emotion.

"Good dinner, babe."

"Uh...Danny, what'd you just eat?"

"Some kind of meat."

"It wasn't just some kind of meat. It was USDA prime sirloin, carefully cut into one-eighth-inch strips, sautéed in creamery butter, smothered in freshly picked mushrooms and dairy sour cream, laced with Cabernet Sauvignon—

1974—and poured over noodles that I made from scratch this morning before you got up."

"Wow, it was really good!"

"Danny, at what point did you realize the incredible taste that you were savoring?"

"I don't know, babe. It was really good. I don't know what time it was. I just know it was good."

"I think maybe if the TV had been off, you would have been more aware."

"Why didn't we turn it off?"

"We didn't turn it off because you put it in the middle of the table and turned it on full blast so you and the kids could watch Doctor Spock, or whatever you call him, beam down for the fifth time this week. But don't worry about it. It's in the past! I'm all over it. It's water under the bridge."

"Well, I'm sorry."

"I'm sorry, too, for thinking you were a complete jackass."

"A jackass?"

"Yeah... and you know when I asked you if you wanted more butter? Well, I almost smeared it over the TV screen and told you to lick it off the *Enterprise*."

"You did?"

"Yeah, but knowing how much we love each other, and knowing I shouldn't take it personally when you gorge down a gourmet meal like a common hog, I found the strength to let it pass."

"Are you calling me a common hog?"

"No, not now. I'm just glad I didn't call you one when you were one."

"Oh."

I had won the fight and made the point that there was a problem. But I had just begun the battle against mealtime television.

That first attempt at weaning my family from the TV had failed. Captain Kirk had won out over the beef Stroganoff, and the spinach soufflé had been unconsciously devoured during a McDonald's commercial. I couldn't totally blame my family, nor could I expect them to change overnight.

The random eating patterns I had allowed them to establish over the years would be hard to correct. It would take at least twenty-one days to change our habits. It was obvious the cold turkey approach was too drastic. I had relied completely on a good meal to entice them to the table, and I couldn't take it personally if my cooking took second place to a TV rerun.

This was a problem that would have to be brought up during the next family council meeting. In our first book, *Sidetracked Home Executives™*, we discussed in depth how to have a weekly family meeting.

To prepare my case, I planned my strategy very carefully. I consulted the local TV listings for the week's most boring nighttime schedule. It looked like a cinch. All I needed was one hour of poor programming in which we could sit down with the TV off, eat leisurely and in peace, and know none of us would feel cheated. In the *TV Guide* it appeared that entire days were boring. I was deluded.

With this problem at the top of the agenda, I discussed at length the time slots that everyone would agree upon. After forty-five minutes of deliberation, we found the only times mutually agreeable were Monday and Wednesday nights from 6:00 to 7 P.M., foregoing *Meet the Mayor, Bowling for Bucks, On Tour with Mel Levart* (travel spelled backward), and *Disease on Parade.*

It was a start. With Monday and Wednesday nights scheduled for the first of many happy dinners, I wanted the menu to be something my family would all enjoy. It was not the night to serve something too healthy, like liver and creamed eggplant, or to dazzle them with a flaming steak Diane and a Caesar salad.

I posted my seven menu cards on my bulletin board so everyone could see what treats were in store. It was obvious my family needed to be more informed. I wanted them to know how I felt. It's no fun to put time and energy into a project and have it go unnoticed and unappreciated. I resented having to tell them how well I'd done. I secretly wished they would naturally understand my side. Couldn't they realize how much thought and work was involved in cooking their meals? Were they insensitive? Couldn't they read my mind?

When was the last time one of my children had come to me and said, "Mommy dearest, how selfish of me to be playing while you prepare our evening meal alone. You get off those precious little feet and let me round up Father and the other children"?

They didn't care. Maybe the best thing I could do would be to take my menus and my recipes and move on down the road. Then what would they do? They wouldn't even miss me until the TV played "The Star-Spangled Banner" and the Reverend Felcher mentioned "daily bread" in his closing prayer.

That first family dinner without TV was like a ten-year class reunion. We renewed old acquaintances as we all discovered that we actually knew each other from somewhere. The conversations were basic.

"Where do you go to school?"

"Hazel Dell."

"Hazel Dell? Wow, I go there, too."

"Yeah? What grade are you in?"

"Third."

"Who's your teacher?"

"Mrs. Sims."

"Hey, I had her last year."

"Yeah?"

But even with all the clever conversation, I still sensed a lack of enthusiasm for the meal. I was confused. The TV had been off, the meal had been great, but nobody had eaten very much. What was wrong?

"Jeff, how come you didn't eat your corn on the cob? Your front teeth have come in."

"I'm full, Mom."

"You didn't eat your buddy burger, either."

"I'm too full, Mom."

"Chris, you love strawberry Jell-O. Do you feel okay?"

"Yeah, but I wasn't very hungry."

"Okay, nobody ate a thing. Were you just too busy getting acquainted? What's the deal?"

"We're full."

"Full? You were starving when you came home from school. What happened?"

The list of what they had eaten between after school and dinnertime was obnoxious. It sounded like what you might find if you pulled out the Hide-A-Bed after five years of using it as the family room sofa: Cocoa Puffs, Tootsie Rolls, Ho-Hos, Hi-Hos, Fruit Loops, KitKats, Yum Yums, Ding Dongs, Twinkies, and bonbons.

It was no wonder they were full. They'd easily consumed fifty dollars worth of junk food since they got home from school. It hadn't been a week since the last one, but I felt an emergency family council meeting was in order. The nutritional value of the snacks would have to change and some rules would have to be set.

I asked everybody for snack suggestions. I wrote down the reasonable ones, such as raw vegetables, fresh fruits, sunflower seeds, raisins, nuts, cheese, and frozen yogurt, and immediately ruled out the unreasonable requests, such as cotton candy, Sno-Kones, and banana splits. I knew I also needed to declare an official time when the kitchen would be closed to all snackers. Four o'clock seemed reasonable, since I planned to have us eat promptly at 6:30. I knew the children needed a good two hours to get hungry again, and I needed that time to prepare the meal in peace. There is nothing more irritating than to try to fix dinner amid a school of landlocked piranhas.

The four o'clock munching curfew officially closed all access to the bread drawer, refrigerator, fruit basket, cupboards, pantry, and freezer. Except for helpers, no one was allowed to set foot onto the kitchen floor.

I realized the importance of enforcing the rule but knew there would have to be exceptions. So I issued two complimentary, nontransferable snack passes (see p. 175 for illustration) to each child per week. They could use the pass in emergencies to relieve the starvation that accompanies after-school sports, ballet lessons, swimming lessons, and yard work. In those hunger emergencies I wasn't too concerned about how close to a meal they used the snack pass. After such strenuous workouts, their appetites returned quickly.

I felt as if I had made progress. Two days a week (eventually to be stretched into seven) we would gather around the table with the TV off. Nutritional snacks would be available after school until 4 P.M. Then only those with snack passes or aprons were allowed access to food.

For once in my life I felt as if I had my family eating on the right track. Things would improve with time, just as everything else in our home had improved. The bottom line was that I was in control of my kitchen and the quality of the meals that I created in it. We were saving money, time, and energy. We had reestablished family communication, and I would be able to help those Sidetracked Home Executives™ who had fallen prey to the tract house and a set of TV trays.

15
THE HEART OF
THE HOME

From Peggy:

In Chapter Ten I shared the experience of having my mouth wired shut after simple surgery to correct an overbite. What I didn't tell you was that I had serious complications that kept me in the hospital for nearly a month.

Our organized little world was turned upside down and everything stopped as we waited for test results and lab reports.

One morning while making his rounds, one of my doctors came in to see me. "Are you bitter?" he asked without warning. "Am I bitter?" I recoiled, unsure of what he meant. "I don't like to think of myself as a bitter person," I said. He sweetly rephrased the question. "Maybe *bitter* is the wrong word. . . . I mean, have you asked yourself why this has happened to you?" I started to cry. I had asked that question over and over again with no answer. I was bitter. I was mad at my body for seeming to let me down. "It just happened," the doctor said quietly, "but now it's up to you, whether or not you get out of here. You have to put it all behind you and let your body heal you." I wasn't sure I

could. In order to do that I would have to give up being
angry. Pain made it hard to think. It was easy to lie there
and be mad, so I did.

Then one day I decided that I wanted to go home! I
missed my family. I missed my Mr. Coffee machine and my
red mug. I wanted to get into my own refrigerator in the
middle of the night. I missed the view from my kitchen
window, and I was ready to start living again.

My body had always done what it was supposed to do
and I'd never had to worry about it, not even through the
births of three babies. It had been years since I'd given any
thought to the miracle of it; the complexity of it; the
simplicity of it; the strength of it.

All of a sudden it failed. With keen interest I started
asking the doctors what my body needed to do to fight the
infection. I found out that each organ was already doing it,
and they were all working together for my survival. It was
amazing... so well thought out. My job was to keep from
interfering with the healing process. That meant guarding
my thoughts and putting any bitterness behind me. It meant
thinking about what I loved and what made me happy.

Pam helped me get better by making me laugh. She'd
visit me, wearing our Captain Ivar mask, tell me funny
things that happened at work, draw me silly pictures, and
read to me from humorous books. Laughing made me forget
about the pain. I couldn't laugh and be depressed at the
same time.

The recovery began with my decision to allow it.

Don't make the mistake of holding onto grudges or harboring
negative feelings about what's happened to you. Whenever
you ask the question "Why me?" you're wasting time and
delaying your recovery. You can learn from every experience if you will put aside the negative and put your
attention on what you can do to help yourself.

When Danny finally brought me home from the hospital,
I went straight to the kitchen to get the feeling that I was
really home. Near the sink, a paper cup filled with dirt had
the name Allyson scrawled across it. A bean plant was
trying to poke through.

I had missed Mom's turkey dinner and egg hunt on Easter, but the kids had saved me the wishbone. It was on the windowsill. Jeff had lost a tooth and it was waiting for me in a glass. Danny wasn't sure how the fairy made the money exchange. The calendar on the bulletin board was a month behind.

There was a note from Chris's teacher, asking me to help with the bike rodeo, and a permission slip for Allyson to visit the fire station.

Danny made me get into bed before I was finished taking it all in. "It's so good to have you back," he said. "Nothing was the same."

I'm well now, and my kitchen is once again bustling with activity. The bean plant had to be moved to the yard, as it was taking over the wet area. The kids are arguing over who gets to be the one to make a wish with me, so the wishbone is still on the windowsill. Jeff has lost another tooth. The fairy gave him his money and paid the I.O.U. The calendar is current, and we've got new menu cards on the bulletin board. Danny helped with the bike rodeo, Allyson visited the fire station, and I am so happy my kitchen is alive again.

From Pam:

Peggy was only supposed to be in the hospital for four days. She had planned everything perfectly. The refrigerator was stocked, the bread was baked, and her menu cards were posted. I went to her house every day to help with the meals, and it was so easy to work in her kitchen. Her wet, hot, cold, and dry areas were just by the book. I thought how neat it was that we had figured out how to organize our kitchens, and the test of how well our system worked was how easily someone else could step in and start cooking.

Her kitchen is so cute. She has a garden window over her sink, and her plants are growing way better than they did when we were slobs. There's a little breakfast nook that she papered in a dusty-red calico print. The sun streams through French doors that open out onto what will someday be a deck. Right now there's about a six-foot dropoff. Her floor is apple-shiny and her counter tops are clear, except for pretty things. She made eyelet curtains out of crisp white cotton and a tablecloth to match.

When the four-day hospital stay turned into a month-long ordeal, Peggy's kitchen began to lose something. Although it was as perfect as a kitchen set in a television studio, and everything was kept just exactly the way she left it, there was an awful void.

Peggy is the happiest person I know. We all felt the terrible emptiness when she was gone. We missed her voice and her impressions of Truman Capote. It has never been so clear to me that life is people, not things, and that somebody can come in and take over the routine but no one can come in and replace a person.

Your kitchen doesn't have to look like one at the home show to be warm and cozy. What it does need is YOU, touching the people around you with your love, your laughter, and your talents. The beautiful YOU. That YOU that is sincere, steadfast, and strong.

Not you sweating and stirring over a hot stove, screaming for help and whining because you don't have a Jenn-Air. Our granny never had a kitchen. She lived in a one-room cabin and her wet, hot, cold, and dry areas were at the north end. We didn't realize the conditions weren't ideal, because Granny acted like they were. She was full of life and contentment. As long as she had her family, a red-checkered tablecloth, an iron frying pan, and a few groceries, she was happy.

Be happy right where you are, regardless of your circumstances, because if you have love, you have everything that matters.

From both of us:

We didn't want this book to be just an organizational manual on kitchen efficiency. We wanted you to laugh with us, because life wasn't meant to be serious or reproduction wouldn't occur the way it does.

We've never claimed to be nutritionists (see Pam and Peggy's Glossary of Nutrition, p. 158). As nutritional fads have tried to infiltrate our thinking, we still follow our inner guidance in preparing nourishing meals. We aren't intimidated by extremists who eat only "natural" foods but choke on bark and die young. We're concerned enough about what we eat to read labels, and we don't buy anything with ingredients we can't pronounce.

Basically, we serve all things in moderation, we use as much fresh food as possible, we've greatly reduced our intake of salt and sugar, we drink eight glasses of water a day, and we exercise and get plenty of rest. We also allow for goodie overindulgences brought on by Trick or Treat, Santa Claus, the Easter Bunny, and Grandma.

There is a lot of technical material here that you may not be ready to use. If the rest of your house is a mess, you might want to take care of that first. Don't worry about how long it will take to get your kitchen clean and organized. It may take you a year to accomplish what some will have time to do in six weeks. Others may spend two years working at it. What counts is that you have a tool you can fall back on anytime you're ready.

Don't get sidetracked and think that getting organized is all that matters in life. You matter, and whether you are organized or not, there is no one else like you. You are the heart of your home and nobody can take your place.

God bless you,
Love,

Pam & Peggy

Pam, Granny, Peggy

We celebrate Mom's and Dad's birthdays on the same day

Peggy and Danny

Crunch-top Char-tots

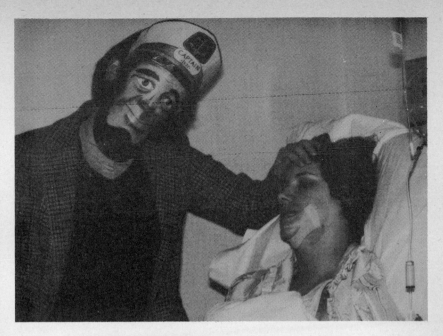

Captain Ivar visiting Peggy after surgery

Pam and Captain Ivar at Christmas

Cooking *with* Gary Collins *on* Hour Magazine

Eating *with* Gary Collins *on* Hour Magazine

APPENDIX

FOODS FOR EVERYDAY

	Ages: 1–3	4–6	7–10	11–teen years	
MEAT GROUP Meat, poultry, fish, organ meats, or meat substitutes	2 servings (1 oz. each)	2 servings (1 1/2 oz. each)	2 servings (1 1/2 oz. each)	2 servings (2–3 oz. each)	Substitutes for the protein of 1 oz. meat: 1 egg, 1 oz. cheese, 1/4 cup cottage cheese, 1/4 cup peanuts or 1/3 cup other nuts, 1/2 cup cooked dry peas or beans, 2 tbsp. peanut butter.
MILK GROUP Milk (whole, skim, dry, evaporated, buttermilk) and other dairy products	2 cups	2 cups	2 cups	3–4 cups (5–6 cups for pregnant teens)	Substitutes for the calcium of 1 cup milk: 1 cup yogurt, 1 1/3 cups cottage cheese, 1 1/2 cups ice cream, 1 1/4 oz. (1/3 cup grated) natural cheese, 1 3/4 oz. process cheese
VEGETABLE-FRUIT GROUP For Vitamin A: deep yellow-orange	4 servings or more (3 tbsp.)	4 servings or more (1/4 cup	4 servings or more (1/3 cup	4 servings or more (1/2 cup	Eat one vitamin C source daily, 1 high vitamin A source at least every other

	each)	each)	each)	each)	
or very dark green For Vitamin C: citrus fruit, melon, strawberries, broccoli, tomatoes, raw cabbage					day. Other fruits and vegetables fill out this food group.
BREAD-CEREAL GROUP Whole grain or enriched bread, cereal, rice, pasta	3 servings	4 servings	4 servings or more	4 servings or more (6 or more for teenage boys)	Very active children, teens, adults, and athletes need more for energy. A serving is 1 slice of bread, 1 roll, 1/2 cup cooked cereal products, or 1 oz. dry cereal.
CALORIE NEEDS	1,300	1,800	2,400	2,400 girls 2,800–3,000 boys	

Adult Needs: Same as teens, except: 2 cups milk, 2,000 calories for women, 2,700 calories for men.
Needs during pregnancy increase.
Serve sweets only after all basic four foods have been eaten.

PAM AND PEGGY'S GLOSSARY OF NUTRITION

Ascorbic Acid—what you get all over yourself when you open an old flashlight

The Basic Seven—a movie starring Clint Eastwood, Telly Savalas, Dean Martin, and Marlon Brando

Caffeine—one of the counselors at Girl Scout camp

Calcium—dishwasher detergent

Calorie—if you don't know what that is, you're probably fat

Carbohydrate—something that falls off of a truck and can be found alongside the freeway

Cyclamates—two people on one bike

Glucose—interior latex enamel

Milligram—pleasant way to keep in touch

Minerals—the black stuff that gets caught in the little round faucet screen

Monosodium Glutamate—an illness that Candy Collins and Hermie Flager spread through Ft. Vancouver High in the spring of '61

Polyunsaturates—waterproof leisure suits

Preservative—something that makes food last longer than you will if you eat it

Protein—advocates of puberty

Starches—a preparation used to stiffen fabrics

Vitamins—Fred, Wilma, Dino, Barney, and Bamm Bamm

Menu-Planning Sheet

Poultry Main Dish	S/S Side	S/S Vegetables	S/S Desserts	Extras	Salads	F/W Side	F/W Vegetables	F/W Desserts

Menu-Planning Sheet

Pork Main Dish	S/S Side	S/S Vegetables	S/S Desserts	Extras	Salads	F/W Side	F/W Vegetables	F/W Desserts

Menu-Planning Sheet

Seafood Main Dish	S/S Side	S/S Vegetables	S/S Desserts	Extras	Salads	F/W Side	F/W Vegetables	F/W Desserts

Menu-Planning Sheet

Lamb Main Dish*	S/S Side	S/S Vegetables	S/S Desserts	Extras	Salads	F/W Side	F/W Vegetables	F/W Desserts

*For Beef Main Dish Menu-Planning Sheet, see p. 45.

Menu-Planning Sheet

Specialties	S/S Side	S/S Vegetables	S/S Desserts	Extras	Salads	F/W Side	F/W Vegetables	F/W Desserts

ACCOMPANIMENT PLANNING SHEET

Side Dishes (potatoes, rice, noodles)	Recipe Source

ACCOMPANIMENT PLANNING SHEET

Vegetables	Recipe Source

ACCOMPANIMENT PLANNING SHEET

Desserts	Recipe Source

ACCOMPANIMENT PLANNING SHEET

Extras	Recipe Source

ACCOMPANIMENT PLANNING SHEET

Salads	Recipe Source

PERSONALIZED GROCERY LIST

MEAT

BEEF

corned beef
hamburger
heart
kidneys
pot roast
roast
short ribs
steak for broiling
steak to marinate
stew meat
tongue

POULTRY

boneless chicken
   breast
chicken giblets
chicken halved
chicken roaster
cornish game hens
fryer parts
turkey
turkey parts

PORK

bacon
Canadian bacon
ham
hot dogs
pork chops
pork roast
pork steaks

PORK (cont.)

pork tenderloin
sausage
spareribs
unseasoned
   ground pork

LAMB

lamb chops
leg of lamb
rack of lamb

SEAFOOD

clams
flounder
halibut
lobster
oysters
red snapper
salmon
scallops
shrimp

CANNED GOODS

clams
fruit
meats
milk
oysters
refried beans
salmon
shrimp
soup

CANNED GOODS
(cont.)

tuna
vegetables

DAIRY PRODUCTS

2% milk
Boursin
butter/margarine
buttermilk
cheddar cheeses
chocolate milk
cottage cheese
cream cheese
eggs
half and half
Jack cheese
powdered milk
sour cream
whipping cream
whole milk
yogurt

FROZEN FOODS

desserts
Dixie cups
French fries
frozen breads
frozen dinners
frozen pizza
fruits
ice cream
pastry cups

FROZEN FOODS
(*cont.*)

pie crusts
Popsicles
pudding sticks
Tater Tots
vegetables

SPICES AND HERBS

basil
bay leaves
celery seed
chili powder
cinnamon
cooking wine
garlic
horseradish
Italian dressing
meat marinade
nutmeg
onion salt
onion soup
oregano
paprika
pepper
poultry seasoning
salt
seasoned salt
soy sauce
sweet and sour
   sauce
Tabasco sauce
taco sauce
teriyaki
vinegar
Worcestershire
   sauce

CONVENIENCE FOODS

biscuit mix
cake mixes
candy bars
cones
corn bread
dip
dry cereal
Jell-O
potato chips
pudding
salad dressings
   (prepared)
tortillas

BAKERY PRODUCTS

brown 'n serve
   rolls
cookies
English muffins
French bread
graham crackers
hamburger buns
Hawaiian bread
hot dog buns
rolls
rye bread
soda crackers
sourdough bread
white bread
whole wheat bread

STAPLES

baking powder
baking soda
bouillon
brown sugar
chocolate chips
cocoa
cornmeal
cornstarch
corn syrup
Dijon mustard
dried beans
flour
honey
ketchup
lemon juice
lentils
maraschino
   cherries
marshmallows
mayonnaise
mustard
noodles
nuts
olive oil
olives
Parmesan cheese
peanut butter
pickles
powdered sugar
rice
shortening
sugar
sunflower seeds
unsweetened
   chocolate
vanilla extract
vegetable oil

PRODUCE

*Fresh Fruits and
    Vegetables*
alfalfa sprouts
apples
apricots
asparagus
bananas
beans
beets
berries
broccoli
brussels sprouts
cabbage
carrots
cauliflower
celery
cherries
corn
cucumber
eggplant
garlic
grapefruit
grapes
lemons
lettuce
melons
mushrooms
onions
oranges
parsley
peaches
pears
peas
peppers
pimientos
pineapple
plums

PRODUCE (cont.)

potatoes
prunes
radishes
sauerkraut
spinach
squash
tomatoes

BEVERAGES

club soda
coffee
juice
soda pop
tea

GENERAL MERCHANDISE

aluminum foil
aspirin
Baggies
bandages
bar soap
bleach
cat food
cellophane tape
charcoal and
    starter fluid
cleanser
conditioner
deodorant
dishwasher
    detergent
dishwashing
    liquid

GENERAL MERCHANDISE (cont.)

dog food
fabric softener
floor wax
freezer paper
furniture polish
garbage bags
kitty litter
laundry detergent
lemon oil
light bulbs
lunch sacks
masking tape
napkins
paper towels
plastic wrap
razor blades
sanitary napkins
shampoo
steel wool pads
tampons
tissues
toilet paper
toothpaste
Ziploc bags

PLACES TO GO

Baskin Robbins
Deli
Eddie's Villa Del
    Weenie
Kentucky Fried
    Chicken
Rendezvous

EXAMPLE OF COMPLETED MENU-PLANNING SHEET

Poultry Main Dish	S/S Side	S/S Vegetables	S/S Desserts	Extras	Salads	F/W Side	F/W Vegetables	F/W Desserts
Fried Chicken	potato salad	corn on cob	apple pie	deviled eggs	pistachio Jell-O	mashed potatoes and gravy	green beans	
Barbecued Chicken	potato salad	corn on cob	Popsicles	seedless grapes	salad bar	potato salad	baked beans	apple pie
Chicken Kiev	rice pilaf	broccoli	tapioca pudding	French bread	fruit salad	rice pilaf	brussels sprouts	chocolate cake
Chicken Teriyaki	noodles	peas	root beer floats	cantaloupe halves	green	rice	stir-fried celery	chocolate pudding
Herb Chicken	stuffing	carrots	candy treats	fruit cup	salad bar	oven-fried potatoes	creamed broccoli	candy treats
Stir-Fried Chicken	Chinese noodles	Chinese vegetables	chocolate pudding	seedless grapes	fruit salad	Chinese noodles	stir-fried vegetables	floats

Crunchy Chicken	potato salad	zucchini Parmesan	Baskin Robbins	deviled eggs	green	scalloped potatoes	zucchini	ice-cream cones
Breasts w/ Pastrami	rice pilaf	green beans	chocolate sodas	apple-sauce	small Caesar	scalloped potatoes	green beans	doughnuts
Roast Turkey	mashed potatoes	green beans	cherry pie	cranberry sauce	pistachio Jell-O	mashed potatoes	green beans	pumpkin pie
Turkey Hindquarters	Dutch potatoes	corn on cob	apple crisp	homemade bread	green	mashed potatoes and gravy	brussels sprouts	ginger-bread
Turkey Breast	camping potatoes	stir-fried vegetables	Jell-O jewels	cranberry sauce	green	stuffing	peas and pearl onions	pumpkin cake
Cornish Game Hens	noodles Italiano	peas and pearl onions	ice-cream sundaes	sour-dough cantaloupe balls	green	stuffing	zucchini	carrot cake
Cornish Game Hens, Barbecued	potato salad	celery and mushrooms	roasted marsh-mallows	barbecued bread	salad bar	mushrooms sautéed	peas	blueberry cobbler

Beef Freezer Card

Rump roast	serves five	#12 8/6/82
Rump roast	serves three	#13 8/11/82
Five N.Y. cut steaks		#14 9/2/82
Five N.Y. cut steaks		#15 9/16/82
Five 1 lb. pkgs. hamburger		#s16, 17, 18, 19, 20 9/18/82
Short ribs	serves five	#21 9/25/82

(pink card)

Crisis Card

#1   Uncooked 9″ x 13″ lasagna 8/7/82
#2   5 stuffed pork chops (browned) 8/12/82
#3   Meatballs for spaghetti 10/17/82
#4   Quart of Navy bean soup 10/21/82
#5   Quart of chili 10/31/82

(pink card)

Snack Pass

This pass entitles

_____
(name)

to enter the kitchen for one (1) snack after the four o'clock curfew.

Nontransferable

PRESSURE COOKING: FAVORITE RECIPES FROM THE SIDETRACKERS' CARD FILE

Main Dishes

PAM AND PEGGY'S CRISIS CASSEROLE

- 1 6 oz. can tuna (or one cup any ground protein)
- 1 cup cheese (you name it)
- 1 can cream of anything soup
- 1 onion, chopped (dehydrated, green or yellow)
- 1 clove garlic (powder's okay)
- ½ cup celery, chopped (If you don't have it, skip it.)
- 2 cups noodles (any shape) or 1½ cups rice (Minute, of course)
- 3 cups seasoned water (Throw in a couple of bouillon cubes or several Frozen Soup Stock Cubes.*)

In a casserole dish sprayed with Pam (no relation to you know who), mix all ingredients. Cover and bake at 375°F for about 45 minutes. The cheese would have been pretty sprinkled on the top, but we should have thought of that before we told you to throw it in the casserole with everything else. If you've got a little more cheese, decorate the top. Serves 5.

*FROZEN SOUP STOCK CUBES

Cover leftover carcass with water. Add favorite seasonings and one sliced onion. Add any wilted but good produce you want to use up and simmer several hours (great room deodorizer). Pour off liquid into ice cube trays and freeze. Collect cubes in a plastic bag for use as needed.

PAM AND PEGGY'S FLASH-IN-THE-PAN ENTREE

2   cups thinly sliced meat strips (chicken, turkey, pork, or beef)
½   cup onion, chopped
½   cup celery, chopped
½   cup anything else green (Frozen vegetables work great.)

Season to taste. Pour into skillet with 2 tablespoons hot oil. Toss to heat through. Serve with noodles or rice. Serves 4.

HAMBURGER PIE

"This recipe is simple, quick, and delicious," writes April Teichrow (our SHE instructor from Milwaukie, OR). "Serve with a salad and a simple dessert. Fantastic for potlucks, too!"

1   lb. ground beef
1   medium onion, chopped
1   can green beans, drained
1   can tomato soup
    Salt and pepper to taste
⅛   tsp. oregano
    Pie crusts for top and bottom, baked

Brown ground beef with onion; drain excess fat. Add green beans, tomato soup, and seasonings. Line a 9" pie pan with bottom crust. Fill with hamburger mixture. Top with upper crust. Flute edges and make a few gashes in center. Bake at 350°F for 25 minutes. Let cool 5 minutes before serving. Serves 6.

DINNER IN A PUMPKIN

(Adapted from *More-a-Mix Cookery*)

1	**medium pumpkin**
2	**lbs. lean ground beef**
½	**tsp. salt**
⅓	**cup celery, chopped**
⅓	**cup onion, chopped**
¼	**cup soy sauce**
2	**tbsp. packed brown sugar**
1	**4 oz. can sliced mushrooms, drained**
1	**10½ oz. can condensed cream of chicken soup**
2	**cups hot cooked rice**

Preheat oven to 375°F. Cut stem end of pumpkin about 3″ around the stem. Cut on a diagonal by slanting knife from outer edge of pumpkin toward center. Reserve top piece. Remove seeds and pulp; discard. Brown ground beef in a pan. Add vegetables and cook until tender. Stir in remaining ingredients and spoon into pumpkin. Replace top of pumpkin. Lightly grease a 10″ circle in center of baking sheet. Place filled pumpkin on greased center. Bake 1 hour until pumpkin is tender. To serve, spoon some of cooked pumpkin and meat filling onto plates. Serves 6–8.

MUCHO CHICKEN BERSERK

Shirlie Byam (Lynnwood, WA) had this winning recipe as her entry in a Mexican cooking contest held in the Seattle area.

    2 tbsp. cooking oil
   12 chicken thighs
   1½ cups dairy sour cream
    ½ cup milk
    1 tsp. salt
    ½ tsp. pepper
    2 tbsp. all-purpose flour
    1 clove garlic
 1 or 2 canned jalapeño peppers
    1 large onion, thinly sliced
    1 4 oz. can diced green chilies
    1 cup (4 oz.) Monterey Jack cheese, shredded

Heat the oil in large frying pan over medium heat. Add chicken and brown well on all sides. While chicken browns, place sour cream, milk, salt, pepper, flour, garlic, and jalapeños in a blender and whirl until smooth. When chicken is brown, transfer to a shallow 3-quart baking dish. Add onion to frying pan and cook just until limp. Spoon onion and green chilies over chicken and pour over the sour cream mixture. Bake, uncovered, in a 350°F oven for 40 minutes or until chicken is tender. Sprinkle with cheese and return to oven for 5 minutes or until melted. Serves 4–6.

TOSTADA QUICHE

9″	pie crust, unbaked
2	green chilies, seeded and chopped
8	oz. ground beef
¼	cup chopped onion
1–2	tbsp. taco seasoning mix
1½	cups (6 oz.) shredded cheddar cheese
3	eggs
1½	cups half-and-half
½	tsp. salt
⅛	tsp. pepper

Preheat oven to 400°F. Bake pastry shell 7 minutes; do not prick. Remove from oven; set aside. Reduce oven temperature to 375°F. In a medium skillet, combine ground beef, onion, green chilies, and taco seasoning mix. Cover and cook until ground beef is browned and onion is tender. Drain. Layer cheese and then ground beef mixture in the pastry shell. In a medium bowl, combine eggs, half-and-half, salt, and pepper. Beat with a fork until well mixed. Pour over ground beef mixture. Bake 45 minutes or until a knife inserted off-center comes out clean. Let stand 10 minutes before serving. Serves 6.

CHICKEN ROMANOFF

A family favorite! Chicken parts and noodles in a delicious cheese sauce. Easy and quick, too. Ready to serve in about half an hour.

1½	lbs. chicken parts
1	cup water
1½	tsp. flour
½	envelope dry onion soup mix
½	cup sour cream
4	tbsp. margarine
	Paprika
	Cayenne pepper
½	cup milk

Wash and dry chicken. Brown in large skillet with 2 tbsp. melted margarine and a generous dash of paprika and cayenne. Combine onion soup mix with water and flour. Add soup mixture to chicken in skillet. Add last 2 tbsp. margarine. Cover pan and reduce heat. Simmer for 15 minutes. Remove chicken to a platter. Mix together milk and cheese packet from Noodles Romanoff. Add this to the pan juices. Blend together and simmer until thickened. Just before serving, add sour cream. Heat through but do not boil. Pass cheese gravy with boiled noodles and chicken parts. Serves 5.

CAROL'S FAVORITE EGG AND SAUSAGE QUICHE

	Pastry for single crust 9" pie
8	oz. bulk pork sausage
4	hard-cooked eggs, chopped
1	cup Swiss cheese, shredded
1	cup cheddar cheese, shredded
3	eggs, beaten
1¼	cups light cream or milk
¾	tsp. salt
⅛	tsp. pepper

Line 9" pie plate with pastry; flute edges. Do not prick. Bake in 350°F oven for 7 minutes. Cook sausage in frying pan; drain well. Sprinkle chopped eggs in bottom of pie shell; top with sausage and cheeses. Combine beaten eggs, milk, salt, and pepper; pour over all. Bake at 350°F for 30–35 minutes or until set. Let stand 10 minutes before serving. Serves 6.

GINA'S DELICIOUS SHRIMP QUICHE

Perfect luncheon dish or dinner, too!

> **Pastry for single crust 9″ pie**
> 8 **oz. Jack cheese, shredded**
> 8 **oz. small shrimp, cooked**
> 3 **eggs**
> 1¾ **oz. can cream of shrimp soup**
> ⅓ **cup milk**
> ¼ **tsp. onion powder**
> ¼ **tsp. garlic powder**
> **About 4 drops Tabasco sauce**
> **Paprika**

Partially bake pastry in a 9″ pie plate at 375°F for 15 minutes. Sprinkle cheese and shrimp into pastry shell. Lightly beat eggs, stir in soup, milk, onion and garlic powder, and Tabasco. Pour into pastry shell. Sprinkle with paprika. Bake at 375°F until set in the center, about 40 minutes. Let stand 10 minutes before cutting. After it is cooked it freezes well. Thaw and reheat. Serves 6.

PAM AND PEGGY'S SWEDISH MEATBALLS

Have your butcher grind together:

> 1 **lb. ground ham**
> 1 **lb. ground pork, unseasoned**
> 1 **lb. ground beef, lean**

Shape into balls the size of large eggs.

Combine in blender jar:

> ½ **fresh pineapple**
> 1 **cup brown sugar**
> ½ **cup vinegar, white**
> 1 **tsp. dry mustard**
> ½ **tsp. salt**
> ½ **tsp. seasoned salt**

Blend and pour over meatballs. Bake, uncovered, at 350°F for 1 hour, basting frequently. They're even tastier reheated the next day. Approximately 24 meatballs.

OLD SWEDISH HAM BALLS

      1   lb. ground ham
    1⅓   lb. ground pork
      1   cup bread crumbs
      2   eggs, well-beaten
      1   cup milk
      1   tsp. dry mustard
      1   cup brown sugar
     ½   cup vinegar
     ½   cup water

Combine meats, bread crumbs, eggs, and milk, mixing thoroughly. Form balls and place in baking pan. Combine remaining ingredients, stir until sugar dissolves, and pour over meatballs. Bake in slow oven at 325°F for 1 hour. Approximately 12 to 15 meatballs.

VERNA DOYLE'S CASSEROLE

      1   lb. lean hamburger, browned
      1   can tomato soup
      1   can string beans (Drain half the liquid.)
            Mashed potatoes

Combine hamburger, soup, and beans and put in casserole. Cover about ¼ inch thick with mashed potatoes. Bake at 350°F for 35 to 40 minutes. Easy and cheap. Serves 6.

VERNA DOYLE'S HOLLYWOOD HASH

1   **pkg. Chinese noodles**
1   **large onion, chopped**
2   **lbs. ground beef**
2   **slices diced bacon, fried till crisp**
1   **pkg. frozen peas**
3   **cans tomato soup**
3   **cans sliced mushrooms**
    Sharp cheddar cheese

Brown ground beef and add diced onion. Cook till soft. Cook noodles until soft and drain. Put noodles in large casserole. Mix ground beef, bacon, tomato soup, peas, and mushrooms together. Grate cheddar cheese and put a generous amount over the top. Bake for 45 minutes at 325°F. Serves 8 or more.

QUICK GRANNY'S DINNER

1   **lb. ground beef**
1   **onion, chopped**
3   **small potatoes, chopped**
3   **tbsp. flour**
1½   **cups water**
     Salt and pepper to taste
     Lawrey's Salt

In skillet brown meat, onions, and potatoes. Season with salt, pepper, and Lawrey's Salt, then sprinkle flour over top. Mix and then add water to make sauce. Cover, and reduce heat, simmering until potatoes are tender and sauce thickens (about 20 minutes). (If you have any leftover vegetables in the refrigerator, add them.) Serves 4.

NOODLES AND LEFTOVER MEAT CASSEROLE

Boil 4 handfuls of noodles and drain
Add:
½   chopped onion
½   cup chopped celery
6   fresh mushrooms, chopped
Leftover meat cut in bite-size pieces (or 1 can of tuna, drained, or crumbled, browned hamburger)
1   pkg. onion and mushroom soup
1   can cream of celery soup
½   cup milk

Bake in covered casserole dish at 350°F for about an hour. Serves 4.

CHICKEN OR TURKEY CASSEROLE

Leftover chicken or turkey (cubed)

1   can cream of chicken and mushroom soup
1   cup small curd cottage cheese
2   stalks celery, chopped
Few fresh mushrooms, sliced
Few water chestnuts, sliced
Stove Top bread crumbs

Mix together and cover top with bread crumbs. Warm in microwave or broil to brown bread crumbs. Serves 4 to 6.

TACO BURGERS

1   lb. ground beef
1   small onion, chopped
¼   cup bread crumbs
1   egg
1   tsp. Worcestershire sauce
⅓   cup green chilies, diced
Salt and pepper
6   corn tortillas

Combine meat, onion, bread crumbs, egg, and Worcestershire. Grill 4 to 6 inches above coals. When meat is done add salt and pepper. Dampen tortillas, stack, and wrap in heavy foil. Place at side of grill to heat. Set out the following condiments: can of heated refried beans, sliced tomatoes, sliced avocados, and taco sauce. Serves 6.

COPALIS CLAM CHOWDER

    12 (or more) razor clams
    ¼   lb. (or a little less) salt pork, chopped
    4   cups water
    4   small potatoes, diced
    ¼   green pepper, chopped
    ½   cup onion, chopped
    1   can condensed milk
    3   tbsp. flour
        Salt and pepper

Dice clams, reserving clam liquor. Fry salt pork, remove, and reserve fat. Add half cup clam liquor and 1½ cups water, potatoes, and onions to fat. Cook covered until potatoes are tender (15 to 20 minutes). Add clams, 1 can of milk, plus 2½ cups water. Blend flour and a little water and stir into chowder. Heat to boil, stirring occasionally. Add seasoning and salt pork. Serves 6.

WINNIE'S MEXICAN DISH

    1   can refried beans
    1   lb. ground beef, browned and drained
    ½   cup Jack cheese, grated
    ½   cup cheddar cheese, grated
    ½   cup mild taco sauce
    ¼   cup green onions, chopped
    ¼   cup guacamole
    1   medium tomato, diced

Line a deep dish with beans. Add beef, cheeses, and put taco sauce over top. Heat in oven at 325°F. Add chopped

green onions, guacamole, and diced tomato. Really good.
Serves 6.

SUSIE'S PIZZA

1   loaf Rhodes Bake N Serve frozen bread dough
1   can Chef Boyardee Pizza Sauce with Cheese
½   lb. ground beef or sausage
1   tbsp. Parmesan cheese
¼   cup cheddar cheese, grated
¼   cup mozzarella cheese, grated
Garlic salt
Oregano

Thaw dough in refrigerator overnight, then divide in half,
cover, and let rise in a warm place until doubled. Roll and
fit each half of the dough into a pizza pan. Spread each
with half of the pizza sauce. Brown the ground beef or
sausage, drain, and spread on the pizzas. Top with cheese,
garlic salt, and oregano to taste. Sprinkle with other favorite
toppings, such as sliced green peppers, pepperoni, or black
olives, if desired. Bake at 450°F until crust is done and
cheese is bubbly. Makes 2 pizzas, approximately 8 servings.

"MAID SERVICE" PANCAKES

Quick and easy! A ready-made pancake and waffle batter to
keep in your refrigerator a week or more. Just pour, grill,
and serve. Great for "busy" mornings.

6   eggs
4   cups buttermilk (1 quart)
¼   cup salad oil
1   cup cream (or canned milk)
1   pkg. dry yeast
4   cups flour
2   tbsp. baking powder
2   tbsp. baking soda
2   tbsp. sugar
1   tsp. salt

Beat eggs. Add buttermilk, salad oil, cream, and yeast. Stir, then add flour, baking powder, baking soda, sugar, and salt. Stir thoroughly. Set in refrigerator overnight. Remove as needed. Bake on hot griddle. Makes 12 servings.

DEE ANNE'S LOW-CAL BLENDER PANCAKES

On a diet? Don't skip breakfast.

> **4   eggs**
> **1   cup cottage cheese**
> **¼   cup flour**
> **1   tsp. sugar**
> **¼   tsp. salt**

Put all ingredients in jar of blender. Blend until smooth. Pour onto a preheated Teflon griddle or surface lightly coated with a low-calorie vegetable spray. Serve with a sprinkle of cinnamon and sugar substitute. Serves 4.

10-MINUTE CLAM CHOWDER

Delicious!

> **1   tsp. onion, grated**
> **3   tsp. butter**
> **1   8 oz. can chopped clams**
> **1½   cups milk**
> **1   cup half-and-half**
> **½   tsp. salt**
> **   Dash ground pepper**
> **1   cup frozen hash brown potatoes**

Melt butter over low heat. Add grated onion and simmer 2 minutes. Add clams and clam liquid. Bring to a boil; add milk. Bring to a simmer again and add hash brown potatoes. Serve with rolls and salad. Serves 4–6.

GREAT STUFF! STUFFING

A tasty change from plain turkey stuffing.

4 tbsp. butter
½ cup onion, chopped
12 ounces spicy/hot sausage meat
Turkey liver, finely chopped
1½ cups dry bread crumbs
½ tsp. thyme
6 tbsp. celery, finely chopped
6 tbsp. parsley, finely chopped
1½ tsp. salt
½ tsp. ground pepper
8 oz. can water chestnuts, chopped
2 apples, peeled and finely chopped
4 tbsp. heavy cream

Melt butter in a heavy skillet; add onions. Sauté until lightly brown. Add sausage meat, breaking it up with a fork as it browns. Transfer entire contents of pan to a fine sieve and let excess fat drain. Add turkey liver to pan and brown quickly. Stir in drained sausage, bread crumbs, thyme, celery, parsley, salt, and pepper. Mix well. Add chestnuts, apple, and heavy cream. Mix well and loosely stuff into turkey cavity. Bake as usual. Stuffing serves 8.

SIDE DISHES

ZUCCHINI CASSEROLE

A real man-pleaser, even for the man in your life who refuses to eat zucchini in anything!

4 medium zucchini, diced (4 cups)
1 medium onion, chopped
½ cup cheddar cheese, grated
1 cup Bisquick mix
1 tsp. salt
1 tsp. pepper
1 tsp. oregano
3 large eggs
½ cup oil

Mix zucchini, onion, cheese, Bisquick, and seasonings in a greased 2-quart casserole. Beat eggs; add oil. Pour over zucchini mixture. Bake uncovered at 350°F for 40 minutes. Serves 6.

ZUCCHINI CASSEROLE II

    2   lbs. zucchini (about 7 medium-size), sliced
    2   small onions, chopped
    ¾   cup chopped celery
    1   can cream of chicken soup
    1   8 oz. carton sour cream
        Salt and pepper to taste
    1   pkg. 8 oz. herb stuffing mix
    ½   cup margarine, melted

Cook zucchini, onions, and celery until half done. Add soup, sour cream, and salt and pepper. Mix well. Combine stuffing mix and margarine, mix well. Put half of stuffing in bottom of casserole, pour in zucchini mix, and sprinkle rest of stuffing on top. Bake for 40 minutes at 350°F. Serves 6–8.

BROCCOLI CASSEROLE

    1   stick butter
    1   onion, chopped
    2   pkgs. frozen chopped broccoli, cooked and drained
    ½   cup Cheese Whiz
    1   cup Minute rice
    ¼   cup milk
    ¼   cup water
    1   can undiluted cream of chicken soup

Sauté onion in butter, add the rest of the ingredients, and bake at 350°F for 35 minutes. Serves 6.

UNCLE CHINK'S BAKED BEANS

Soak 2 cups white navy beans overnight in bean pot.
Next morning add:

4   heaping tbsp. brown sugar
4   tsp. mustard
Pepper and salt
1   onion, chopped
2   pork steaks, cut up in cubes

Bake at 300°F with cover on for 4 hours. Serves 8.

RICE SOUFFLÉ

3   eggs, separated
1   cup cold cooked rice (leftover or cooked and cooled)
2   tbsp. butter
½   cup milk
¼   pound cheddar cheese, grated
Pinch of salt

Beat egg whites until stiff. Add egg yolks to cold rice. Blend
in butter, milk, and grated cheese. Stir well. Gently fold in
beaten egg whites. Salt to taste. Bake in a greased casserole
at 300°F for 30–45 minutes or until brown on top. Serves
4–6.

SALADS

BEET SALAD

Here's a really tasty gelatin salad with a surprising ingredient—beets.

- 1   **8 oz. can crushed pineapple**
- 1   **1-lb. can julienne-style beets**
- 1   **3 oz. pkg. raspberry gelatin**
- ½   **cup nuts, chopped**
- 3   **tbsp. lemon juice**
- ¼   **cup white vinegar**
- 2   **tbsp. sugar**
     Mayonnaise or sour cream

Drain and save juice from beets and pineapple. Add enough water to juice to make 1½ cups liquid. Add lemon juice, vinegar, and sugar. Bring to a boil and add to gelatin. Stir to dissolve. Add drained pineapple, beets, and nuts. Pour into a 3-quart-size mold. Chill until firm. Unmold. Serve with mayonnaise or sour cream. Serves 6–8.

THE SALAD BAR

Chopped—lettuce
    scallions
    beets
    radishes
    mushrooms
    hard-boiled eggs

Shredded—cheese
    carrots

Sliced—tomatoes
    olives
    avocados
cottage cheese
5-bean salad
croutons
pickles
bean sprouts
water chestnuts
sunflower seeds

DORA'S SWEET AND SOUR CARROT SALAD

  2   lbs. carrots, sliced and cooked (until barely cooked)
  1   small onion, sliced
  1   small bell pepper, sliced

Mixture:

  1   can tomato soup
  1   cup sugar
 ¾   cup vinegar
 ½   cup oil
 ½   tsp. celery seed
  1   tsp. Worcestershire sauce
 ½   tsp. prepared mustard
 ⅛   tsp. salt

Blend mixture well (in blender), add to sliced carrots, onions, and pepper. Store in refrigerator in covered dish or jar. Better if made about 2 days ahead and allowed to marinate. Serves 6–8.

MOLDED SALAD—VERNA DOYLE

1   pkg. lemon Jell-O
2   cups boiling water
1   cup blanched almonds
2   cups small curd cottage cheese
1   cup celery, diced
1   cup apples, diced
1   can pineapple tidbits
2   tbsp. salad dressing
2   tbsp. cream
1½ cups powdered sugar

Dissolve Jell-O in water and cool, until it starts to thicken, then add the rest of the ingredients. Refrigerate until thickened. Serves 8.

DESSERTS

APPLE CRUMBLE

A quick 'n easy dessert. Always receives compliments! Pop it in the oven as you serve dinner. Spoon onto dessert plates while piping hot, and top with a scoop of vanilla ice cream or cream.

1   quart apples, peeled and sliced
1¼   cups light-brown sugar
6   shakes of cinnamon
¼   cup water
⅓   cup butter or margarine
1   cup flour
1   tsp. salt

Place apples in a buttered baking dish. Add ¾ cup brown sugar, water, and cinnamon. Blend flour, ½ cup brown sugar, salt, and butter to make crumbly mixture. Spread this over apples. Bake at 350°F for about 50 minutes. Serves 6.

DRAMATIC ELEGANT DESSERT

Put one sugar cube for each serving in a small dish. Pour lemon extract over cubes to saturate. Put one scoop vanilla ice cream in serving dish (stemware is dramatic). Place saturated cube on top, dim lights, and ignite sugar cube. Serve immediately.

WAFFLE COOKIES

Great idea for fast, fun chocolate cookies. They're made in a waffle iron!

- ½ cup butter or margarine
- 6 tbsp. unsweetened cocoa
- ¾ cup sugar
- 1 cup flour
- 1 tsp. vanilla
  Dash of salt
- 2 large eggs

Melt butter or margarine in saucepan. Add other ingredients. Blend together. Drop by tablespoons on pre-heated waffle iron. Bake 1 minute. (If desired, frost with a mixture of: 3 tablespoons hot water, 2 heaping tablespoons cocoa, a dash of salt, and enough powdered sugar for desired consistency.) Makes 2 dozen cookies.

NO-BAKE PUMPKIN PIE

No room in the oven? Try this light, chiffon-style pie.

- 8" pre-baked pie shell
- 1 pkg. Jell-O instant vanilla pudding
- 1 cup prepared Dream Whip
- 1 cup canned pumpkin
- ½ cup milk
- ¼–½ tsp. each of the following spices: nutmeg, ginger, cinnamon, ground clove

Combine ingredients. Beat slowly, just to blend. Chill in the pie shell. Serves 6.

FAST, FAST FUDGE

For many families homemade fudge is a tradition at the
holidays, but if you traditionally don't have time, try this
recipe for microwave ovens.

    1 lb. confectioners' sugar
    ½ cup cocoa
    ¼ cup milk
    ¼ lb. butter or margarine
    1 teaspoon vanilla
    ½ cup chopped nuts

Lightly grease an 8″ square dish. Place confectioners' sugar
and cocoa in a medium-size, flame-resistant, nonmetallic
mixing bowl. Stir to combine. Add milk and butter to
sugar-cocoa mixture. *Do not stir.* Heat uncovered on full
power, 2 minutes. Stir until blended. Pour into prepared
dish and refrigerate 1 hour before cutting and serving.
Great for gifts, too! Makes approximately 2 dozen pieces.

PEANUT BUTTER FINGERS

A very tasty and quick treat for snacking. It's from a cook
booklet called "Cookin' with Nothin" by Alice B. Davenport.

    6 slices day-old bread
    4 tbsp. margarine
    5 tbsp. peanut butter
    ¾ tsp. cinnamon
    5 tbsp. sugar

Cut bread into three strips per slice. Melt margarine in a
small saucepan; stir in peanut butter. Heat to very warm.
Coat bread with mixture. Combine cinnamon and sugar;
roll fingers in this. Place on an ungreased cookie sheet.
Bake at 350°F for 8 minutes, turn and bake 2 minutes
longer. Makes 18 fingers.

GRASSHOPPER PIE

A family favorite. (We suggest you make two and keep one in the freezer for unexpected guests.)

Crust:
- 16 Oreo cookies
- 4 tbsp. butter, melted

Crush cookies in a blender. Add to melted butter. Shape into bottom of a greased 9″ pie plate. Freeze to set.

Filling:
- 24 large marshmallows
- ⅔ cup milk
- ¼ cup crème de menthe (green)
- 2 tbsp. white crème de cacao
- 1 cup heavy cream, whipped

Melt marshmallows in milk in a double boiler. When melted, remove from heat and cool. Add liqueurs and fold in whipped cream. Pour into crust. Freeze until ready to serve. Serves 6.

OVERNIGHT CRUNCH COFFEE CAKE

This recipe was tastefully submitted by Peggy Angell (Seattle, WA) for our newsletter, *The Locomotivator*.

2 **cups sifted flour**
1 **tsp. baking powder**
1 **tsp. baking soda**
1 **tsp. cinnamon**
½ **tsp. salt**

⅔ **cup butter or margarine**
1 **cup sugar**
½ **cup brown sugar, firmly packed**
2 **eggs**
1 **cup buttermilk**

½ **cup brown sugar, firmly packed**
½ **tsp. cinnamon**
¼ **tsp. nutmeg**
½ **cup chopped walnuts**

Sift first five dry ingredients. Cream butter or margarine and sugar until light and fluffy. Add eggs, one at a time, beating well after each. Alternately mix dry ingredients and buttermilk to the creamed mixture. Spread batter in a greased and floured 13″ x 9″ x 2″ pan. In a small bowl, combine final four ingredients. Sprinkle over batter. Refrigerate 8 hours or overnight. Bake at 350°F for 35–40 minutes or until done. Cut into squares and serve warm. Yield: 16 servings.

GINGERBREAD BOYS

Put a little ball of dough under each cookie's waistline area for pudgy little bellies.

¼	**cup shortening**
½	**cup sugar**
½	**cup dark molasses**
¼	**cup water**
2½	**cups flour**
¾	**tsp. salt**
½	**tsp. baking soda**
¾	**tsp. ginger**
¼	**tsp. nutmeg**
⅛	**tsp. allspice**

Mix shortening and sugar thoroughly. Add molasses and water; continue to mix. Combine dry ingredients and add to molasses mixture. Chill dough 2–3 hours. Roll dough on a lightly floured board to ¼" thickness. Cut shapes with gingerbread boy cutter dipped in flour. Bake on a lightly greased baking sheet at 375°F for 10–12 minutes. Makes about 15 large gingerbread boys.

DEE ANNE'S BUTTER COOKIES

1	**cup butter or margarine**
½	**cup sifted powdered sugar**
1	**egg**
1	**tsp. vanilla**
3	**cups sifted flour**
1	**tsp. baking soda**
1	**tsp. cream of tartar**
½	**teaspoon salt**

Cream butter or margarine. Gradually add powdered sugar. Mix until fluffy. Add egg and vanilla. Sift together dry ingredients. Gradually add to creamed mixture and combine into a ball. Roll on lightly floured surface to ⅛" thickness. Cut into shapes. Bake 10–12 minutes at 375°F. Decorate when cool. Makes 4–6 dozen cookies.

FRUIT LEATHER

> **10   cups ripe fruit, peeled and sliced (peaches,
>   apricots, strawberries)**
> **1   cup sugar**

Put ingredients into a large saucepan. Bring to boil, stirring
until sugar is dissolved. In several small batches, puree
fruit in a blender jar. Pour out puree ¼" thick onto a baking
sheet tautly covered with plastic wrap. On a sunny day, dry
in the hot, bright sun. Bring inside at the end of the day;
continue drying in a 150°F oven. The puree will peel easily
when finished. Roll it up on its plastic; wrap in a plastic
bag. Seal tightly. It will keep one month at room temperature,
four months in the refrigerator, and one year in the freezer.
(Note: To keep bugs away while drying, suspend a tent of
cheesecloth over the baking sheet.) Approximately 20 snacks.

HOT FRUIT COMPOTE

Perfect with ham.

> **1   can sliced peaches**
> **1   can pears**
> **1   can pineapple chunks**
> **1   can apples, cubed**
> **1   can cherry pie filling (thickened, ready to use)
>   (All cans #303 or 1 lb. approximately)**

Mix well with fingers: 1 cup brown sugar, 2 tbsp. cornstarch, and scant ½ tsp. curry powder. Lay fruit in order
given and sprinkle each layer with sugar mixture. End with
top layer of cherries. Dot with butter. Bake 1 hour at 350°F.
Serves 8–10.

FINGER JELL-O

3   small pkgs. Jell-O
4   cups boiling water
4   pkgs. gelatin, unflavored
2   tbsp. lemon juice

Dissolve Jell-O and gelatin in water. Add lemon juice. Chill, cut in any shape. Serves 12.

EXTRAS

MUFFINS REUBEN

4   English muffins, split and toasted
8   slices corned beef
1   cup sauerkraut, drained
8   slices Swiss cheese
Mustard

Spread muffin halves with mustard, top with corned beef, sauerkraut, and cheese, place on baking sheet and broil until cheese melts. Makes 4–8 servings.

ZUCCHINI BREAD

4   cups zucchini, cubed
4   eggs
½   cup vegetable oil
1   cup walnuts (optional)
3   cups all-purpose flour
3   cups sugar
2   tsp. cinnamon
2   tsp. baking powder
1   tsp. baking soda
½   tsp. salt
1   12-ounce pkg. chocolate chips
1   tsp. vanilla extract

Put zucchini cubes, eggs, and oil in a blender. Blend at high speed until mixture is finely pureed. Small green flecks will be visible. Add walnuts, if desired, and blend briefly to chop. Set aside. In a large bowl, mix flour, sugar, cinnamon, baking powder, baking soda, and salt. Add blended zucchini mixture. Stir just enough to moisten dry ingredients. Fold in chocolate chips and vanilla. Pour batter into a buttered tube pan or 2″ x 9″ x 5″ bread loaf pan. Bake at 350°F for about 1 hour. When done, cake tester inserted into middle of loaf will come out clean. Serves 8.

BEER BREAD

Your husband will be impressed that you made homemade bread from scratch! He will think you slaved all day in the kitchen, and he will rave about it every time you make it...and it's so simple and easy.

    3   **cups self-rising flour**
    2   **tbsp. sugar**
    1   **12 oz. can beer**

By hand, mix until dry ingredients are just blended into beer. Pour into well-greased bread pan. Bake at 375°F (350°F if you use a glass pan) for 1 hour. Serve warm. Goes great with pot roast, chili, and stew. Makes delicious toast the next morning, too. Makes one loaf.

FREEZER BREAD

    18   **cups flour**
    ¾   **cup sugar or honey**
    3   **tbsp. salt**
    4   **pkgs. active dry yeast**
    6   **tbsp. melted margarine, or oil**
    6¾   **cups warm water (110°F)**

Mix together ⅓ of all the flour, sugar (if used), salt, and yeast in a large mixing bowl. Add the oil (or margarine) and honey (if used), then gradually stir in the water. Add another ⅓ of the flour, a little at a time, stirring vigorously after each addition. With your hands or a spoon, work in remaining flour, one cup at a time. Turn dough out onto a floured board and knead until smooth and satiny (about 10 minutes). Dough should be on the soft side. Divide into 6 equal portions (about 1½ lb. each) and knead each as you shape into a smooth loaf. Place on a greased baking sheet—3 per sheet, making sure sides don't touch. Cover tightly with clear plastic and freeze. When firm, wrap each one separately in plastic and foil. Place in plastic bags and return to freezer; use within 6 weeks.

To thaw: Remove desired loaves, unwrap. Grease loaf pan and bread well with margarine (no oil). Place in oven on rack with a bowl or pan of boiling water on the bottom. Leave overnight to rise (about 8 hours).

Bake in 375°F oven for 30–35 minutes or until golden brown and hollow-sounding when tapped. Cool on rack after removing from pans. Swish tops with butter if a soft crust is desired.

Makes six loaves of homemade bread to thaw and bake as needed over the next month and a half.

BAR-B-Q SAUCE

  1   tsp. chili powder
  1   tbsp. Worcestershire sauce
  1   tbsp. shortening
  2   tbsp. vinegar
  2   tbsp. brown sugar
  ¼   cup fresh or frozen pure lemon juice
  ¼   cup onion, grated
  ½   cup water
  1   cup chili sauce (do not substitute)

In a large saucepan combine all ingredients and cook over medium heat for 20 minutes.

Baste spareribs or chicken. Extra sauce can be stored in refrigerator or freezer. Makes enough to baste 8 lbs. of meat.

FOR THE BIRDS...WINTER FOOD

> 1   lb. lard
> 12 oz. jar crunchy peanut butter
> 1   lb. melted suet

Put all of the above ingredients into a double boiler and stir together. When thoroughly melted and mixed, pour this mixture over the following dry ingredients, which have been put into a large pan:

> 2   lbs. (12 oz. pkg.) yellow cornmeal
> 10 lbs. wild bird seed

Mix all together and pour into containers. Use large cake pans and put into squares or smaller containers, such as small cottage cheese containers, tuna cans, etc. Wrap the "cakes" in wax paper or foil and refrigerate. Pine cones can be used by pushing this mixture inside the cones. Hang "cakes" or cones from a free limb or in a bird feeder. Serves about 731 birds.

HOMEMADE MAYONNAISE

Made in a blender it's a mini, but big on rave reviews.

> 1   egg
> 5   tsp. lemon juice
> 1   tsp. dry mustard
> ¾   tsp. salt
> ¼   tsp. white pepper
> 1   cup salad oil

In a blender, combine and blend together all ingredients, *except* salad oil, at highest speed. With blender on at highest speed, pour salad oil in a slow and steady stream. By the end of adding the oil, mixture should be thick and creamy. Store in a covered container in the refrigerator. Makes 1 cup.

ORANGE JULIUS

Quick and easy. A refreshing ice-cold treat for a hot summer day! Submitted by Peggy Ann Brace, age 10.

    1   6 oz. can orange juice
    1   cup milk
    1   cup water
    ½   cup sugar
    1   tsp. vanilla extract
        Ice cubes

Mix ingredients in blender until they reach a slushy consistency. Makes enough for 4 tall glasses.

GARLIC MARINADE

    ½   cup salad oil
    ¼   cup red wine vinegar
    ¼   cup lemon juice
    1   tbsp. instant minced onion
    2   cloves garlic, pressed
    ½   tsp. salt
    ½   tsp. pepper

VERNA DOYLE'S CHINESE MUSTARD

    1   tbsp. dry mustard
    ½   tsp. salt
    ½   tsp. cayenne pepper
    2   tsp. vinegar
    ¼   cup light cream

Blend seasonings with vinegar, mixing well till smooth. Add cream. Hot but good—for Chinese pork.

HOLIDAY BEVERAGES

When guests arrive, refreshing beverages are frequently offered. Here are two recipes, one hot and one cold, you can make quickly and easily.

HOT SPICED PERCOLATOR PUNCH

In a party-size coffee pot (24–30 cups) combine 9 cups of unsweetened pineapple juice, 9 cups cranberry juice cocktail, 4½ cups water, and 1 cup brown sugar. In the basket assembly place 4½ tsp. whole cloves, 4 cinnamon sticks— broken in pieces—and ¼ tsp. salt. Assemble, plug in, and perk. Serve piping hot. Approximately 22 servings.

CARIL SCOTT'S FAVORITE PUNCH

"It's a great look-alike for non-alcohol drinkers!"
Combine 2 quarts of white Welch's Grape Juice and 1 quart ginger ale. Cheers! to Caril Scott (Seattle, WA). Approximately 12 servings.

STRAWBERRY SMOOTHIE

A recipe from *Parent Tricks-of-the-Trade* by Kathleen Touw.

- **1   banana**
- **1   pkg. frozen strawberries**
- **1   quart milk**

Combine everything in a blender. Delicious! Makes 4 servings.

EDIBLE PLAY-DOH

Another recipe from Kathleen Touw's *Parent Tricks-of-the Trade*. This one is from the "Art, Crafts and Activities" chapter.

- **1   cup peanut butter**
- **½   cup powdered milk**
- **½   cup wheat germ**
- **¼   cup honey**

Stir together. If sticky, add more milk powder. Decorate with raisins, coconut, vegetable sticks, bean sprouts, or red hot candies. For children 18 months–7 years. Fun enough for 4.

Pam and Peggy present mini workshops for churches, clubs and conventions throughout the country. If you are interested in obtaining more information or would like to order the complete home study course on cassette tapes and/or subscribe to the bi-monthly newsletter, *She's On Track,* write or call:

Sidetracked Home Executives™, Inc.
P.O. Box 5364
Vancouver, Washington 98668
(206) 696-4091

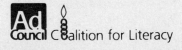